Corner stones

CANADIAN LANGUAGE ARTS

Anthology 6a

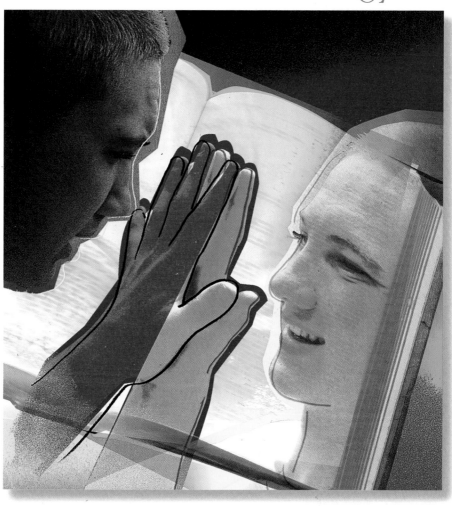

gagelearning

National Library of Canada Cataloguing in Publication Data

Main entry under title:

Gage cornerstones: Canadian language arts. Anthology,

Writing team: Christine McClymont, et al.
ISBN 0-7715-1216-3

1. Readers (Elementary).   I. McClymont, Christine.
II. Title: Cornerstones: Canadian language arts.
III. Title: Anthology, 6a

PE1121.G27 1998   428.6   C98-932139-8

Researchers: Monika Croydon, Monica Kulling, Todd Mercer

Cover Illustration: Kevin Ghiglione

Acknowledgments

Every reasonable effort has been made to trace ownership of copyrighted material. Information that would enable the publisher to correct any reference or credit in future editions would be appreciated.

We acknowledge the financial support of the Government of Canada through the Book Publishing Industry Development Program for our publishing activities.

We acknowledge the government of Ontario through the Ontario Media Development Corporation's Ontario Book Initiative.

7 "the drum" from *Spin a Soft Black Song* by Nikki Giovanni. © 1971, 1985 by Nikki Giovanni. Reprinted by permission of Farrar, Straus & Giroux, Inc. / **8-11** "Kids Speak Out!" by Catherine Rondina. Statistics courtesy of *Chatelaine* magazine. © McLean Hunter Publishing, Ltd. / **14** "When I Grow Up" from *A Pizza the Size of the Sun* by Jack Prelutsky. © 1994, 1996 by Jack Prelutsky. By permission of Greenwillow Books, a division of William Morrow & Company, Inc. / **16-23** "Water Spirit" from *Cloudwalker: Contemporary Native American Stories* by Joel Monture. Reprinted with permission. © 1996 by Joel Monture. Fulcrum Publishing, Inc., Golden, CO. All rights reserved. / **26-27** "Why Do Things Have to Change?" from *It's All Down Hill From Here* by Lynn Johnston. © by Lynn Johnston Productions Inc./Dist. by United Feature Syndicate, Inc. / **30-35** "Rachel and Nathan" from *Finding a Way* by Maxine Rosenberg. Photographs © 1988 by George Ancona. By permission of Lothrop, Lee & Shepard Books, a division of William Morrow & Company, Inc. Text © 1988 by Maxine Rosenberg. Reprinted by permission of the author. / **38** "Yesterday" from *Hey World, Here I Am!* by Jean Little. Used by permission of Kids Can Press, Ltd., Toronto. © 1986 by Jean Little. / **40-45** "The New Moon and the Rain Horn" by Gaele Sobott-Mogwe from *The River That Went to the Sky.* © 1995 by Kafiya Nakaka Phini. / **49** "Prayer for Earth" from *Flights of Fancy* by Myra Cohn Livingston. © 1993, 1994 by Myra Cohn Livingston. "Prayer for Earth" first appeared in *The Big Book for Our Planet* (Dutton). By permission of Marian Reiner. / **50-51** "Four Friends Save Sheep" from *Wild Magazine* (July 1997). © 1997 by Douglas Cowell. / **52-53** "Timberrrr!" excerpt from *Take Action* by Ann Love and Jane Drake, used by permission of the authors. © 1992 by Ann Love and Jane Drake. / **56-61** "How Monkeys Make Chocolate" adapted from *How Monkeys Make Chocolate* by Adrian Forsythe. © 1995 by Adrian Forsythe. With permission of the publisher, Greey de Pencier Books, Inc., Toronto. / **64** "Those Eyes" from *Sawgrass Poems: A View of the Everglades.* © 1996 by Frank Asch, by permission of Harcourt Brace & Company. / **66-75** "Tiktala" by Margaret Shaw-MacKinnon. Text © 1996 by Margaret Shaw-MacKinnon. Illustrations © 1996 by László Gál. Reprinted with permission of Stoddart Publishing Co., Ltd. / **80-83** "Oil and Water Don't Mix" from *Anatomy of an Oil Spill* in *Wild Magazine* (May/June 1996) / **86-89** "Tell the World" from *Tell the World: A Young Environmentalist Speaks Out* by Severn Cullis-Suzuki. Text © 1993 by Severn Cullis-Suzuki. Illustrations by the students of the Etobicoke School of the Arts. Reproduced with the permission of Doubleday Canada Ltd. / **93** "Fantasia" from *A Sky Full of Poems* by Eve Merriam.

© 1964, 1970, 1973, 1986 by Eve Merriam, 1998 by Dee Michel and Guy Michel. Used by permission of Marian Reiner. / **94-99** "The Fight" by Sigmund Brouwer. © by Sigmund Brouwer. Reprinted with permission of the author. / **102-103** "Tales for Peace" excerpted from *Peace Tales: World Folktales to Talk About.* © 1992 by Margaret Read MacDonald. Reprinted by permission of Linnet Books/The Shoe String Press, Inc., North Haven, CT. / **106-109** "Letters from Baghdad" by Barbara Bedway from *On the Wings of Peace*, edited by Sheila Hamanaka. © 1995 by Barbara Bedway. Compilation © by Sheila Hamanaka. Reprinted by permission of Clarion Books/Houghton Mifflin Company. All rights reserved. / **112** "The Paint-Box" by Tali Shurek. © 1975 by Sabra Books, Tel Aviv. / **113** "War Is Here" by students from Zenica, Bosnia-Hercegovina. © 1995 by Paul Fleischman. Used by permission of HarperCollins Publishers. / **114-119** "The Story of In Flanders Fields" from *In Flanders Field: The Story of the Poem* by John McCrae. Text © by Linda Granfield. Illustrations © by Janet Wilson. Reprinted with permission of Stoddart Kids, Ontario. / **122-131** "Sadako" by Eleanor Coerr, illustrated by Ed Young. Text © 1977 by Eleanor Coerr. Illustrations © 1993 by Ed Young. Used by permission of G.P. Putnams Sons, a division of Penguin Putnam Inc. / **134** "In the Next War" by Robert Priest. © by Robert Priest. / **138-139** "Zeke McPeake" and "We're Loudies!" from *A Pizza the Size of the Sun* by Jack Prelutsky. © 1994, 1996 by Jack Prelutsky. By permission of Greenwillow Books, a division of William Morrow & Company, Inc. / **142-143** "Too Young For This; Too Old For That!" by Peg Kehret. © 1986 by Meriwether Publishing Ltd. / **146-149** "Nitro" by Patrick Watson and John Herd Thompson. Text and Images of Heritage Minute reprinted by permission of the CRB Foundation. / **152-157** "The Tiger's Whisker" by Sylvia Sikundar. © 1996 by Sylvia Sikundar.

Photo Credits

4, 56 Frans Lanting/Minden Photos; **9-10, 85 top, bottom, 140** Dave Starrett; **29** Ed Eng; **50** Y. Momatiuk/ Animals, Animals; **50 inset** Douglas Cowell; **55 top** Rich Frishman/Tony Stone Images, **bottom** Chip Porter/Tony Stone Images; **57 background** Frans Lanting/Tony Stone Images, **inset** Wolfgang Bayer; **58** N.H. Dan Cheatham/DRK Photo; **59** Haraldo Castro; **60** Chocolate Association; **61** Russel A. Mittermeier; **62** Mike DoBel/Masterfile; **76** Corel Stock Photo Library; **77 left, right** John de Visser/Masterfile, **middle** Paul von Baich/First Light; **78, 79 left, right** Jan Becker; **80** J.B. Diederich/First Light; **81** Huw Evans/AP Photo; **82-83** Jurgen Burkard/First Light; **82 inset** Jim Zuckerman/First Light; **83 inset** Kennan Ward; **86** Barbara Woodley; **91 top** Paul Bailey Photography, **middle** © Dr Patrick Gregory, **bottom** © David Bird; **111** Toronto Star/P. Power; **120, 121** Guelph Museums: McCrae House; **132** Sadako Project/Informed Democracy

Illustrations

6-7, 100 Susan Todd; **9-10** Margo Davies Leclair; **13, 55** Jun Park; **25, 101, 144-145** Dayle Dodwell; **28, 133** Dan Hobbs; **37, 104, 105,**

Cornerstones Development Team

HERE ARE THE PEOPLE WHO WORKED HARD TO MAKE THIS BOOK EXCITING FOR YOU!

WRITING TEAM

Christine McClymont
Patrick Lashmar
Dennis Strauss
Patricia FitzGerald-Chesterman
Cam Colville
Robert Cutting
Stephen Hurley
Luigi Iannacci
Oksana Kuryliw
Caroline Lutyk

GAGE EDITORIAL

Joe Banel
Rivka Cranley
Elizabeth Long
David MacDonald
Evelyn Maksimovich
Diane Robitaille
Darleen Rotozinski
Jennifer Stokes
Carol Waldock

GAGE PRODUCTION

Anna Kress
Bev Crann

DESIGN, ART DIRECTION & ELECTRONIC ASSEMBLY

Pronk&Associates

ADVISORY TEAM

Connie Fehr Burnaby SD, BC
Elizabeth Sparks Delta SD, BC
John Harrison Burnaby SD, BC
Joan Alexander St. Albert PSSD, AB
Carol Germyn Calgary B of E, AB
Cathy Sitko Edmonton Catholic SD, AB
Laura Haight Saskatoon SD, SK
Linda Nosbush Prince Albert SD, SK
Linda Tysowski Saskatoon PSD, SK
Maureen Rodniski Winnipeg SD, MB
Cathy Saytar Dufferin-Peel CDSB, ON
Jan Adams Thames Valley DSB, ON
Linda Ross Thames Valley DSB, ON
John Cassano York Region DSB, ON
Carollynn Desjardins Nipissing-Parry Sound CDSB, ON
David Hodgkinson Waterloo Region DSB, ON
Michelle Longlade Halton CDSB, ON
Sharon Morris Toronto CDSB, ON
Heather Sheehan Toronto CDSB, ON
Ruth Scott Brock University, ON
Elizabeth Thorn Nipissing University, ON
Jane Abernethy Chipman & Fredericton SD, NB
Darlene Whitehouse-Sheehan Chipman & Fredericton SD, NB
Carol Chandler Halifax Regional SB, NS
Martin MacDonald Strait Regional SB, NS
Ray Doiron University of PEI, PE
Robert Dawe Avalon East SD, NF
Margaret Ryall Avalon East SD, NF

3

Contents

❋ Canadian Content

the drum

POEM BY *Nikki Giovanni*

daddy says the world is
a drum tight and hard
and i told him
i'm gonna beat
out my own rhythm

In this article, you'll read about the results of a survey of kids' opinions. As you read, compare your own opinions with those of other Canadian kids. Remember, you may not necessarily agree with the findings.

Magazine Article by
CATHERINE RONDINA *and* **SARMISHTA SUBRAMANIAN**

Photos by
DAVE STARRETT

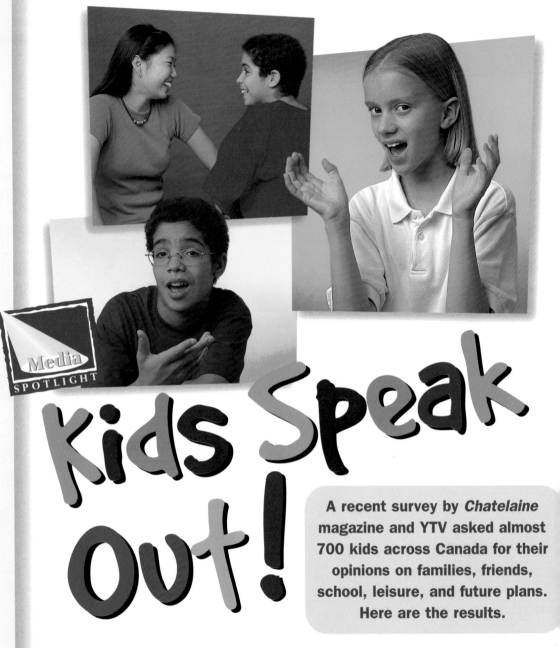

Kids Speak Out!

A recent survey by *Chatelaine* magazine and YTV asked almost 700 kids across Canada for their opinions on families, friends, school, leisure, and future plans. Here are the results.

NICE KIDS

Is it good to be bad? Canadian kids don't think so (though many of their favourite TV characters are bad). According to the survey, eight out of ten kids (that's 80%) describe themselves as **nice**, and 57% say they would give money to a homeless person on the street.

"I'd probably give them a dollar or two," says one boy.

Canadian kids are honest, too, and they say they trust each other. One question asked kids what they thought their friends would do if they found a neat watch in the schoolyard. Six out of ten said their friends would be honest and turn it in.

HOME LIFE

Who's in charge? Most kids (two out of three) say their parents are in charge at home, and it's OK with them. About 40% of eleven- and twelve-year-olds still have TV-viewing rules set by parents. Kids say both parents make important family decisions, but if their parents are talking about divorce, half of all kids say they want to be in on the discussions.

SCHOOL'S COOL!

Is it cool to stay in school? Seven out of every ten kids answering the survey say "Yes!" These kids plan to go on to university. More girls than boys say they plan to get a higher education. Girls are also more likely to say that school is fun.

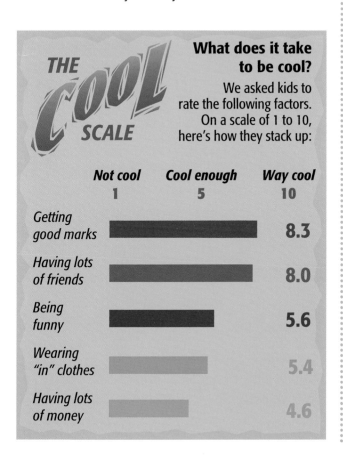

THE COOL SCALE

What does it take to be cool?
We asked kids to rate the following factors. On a scale of 1 to 10, here's how they stack up:

	Not cool 1	Cool enough 5	Way cool 10
Getting good marks			8.3
Having lots of friends			8.0
Being funny			5.6
Wearing "in" clothes			5.4
Having lots of money			4.6

Looking ahead to the future after graduation, most boys plan careers in the world of sports, police work, the arts, or medicine. Most girls, on the other hand, plan careers in teaching, the arts, veterinary science, or medicine.

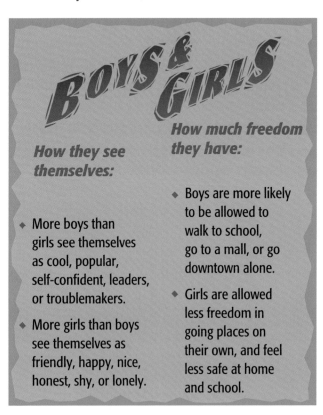

BOYS & GIRLS

How they see themselves:

- More boys than girls see themselves as cool, popular, self-confident, leaders, or troublemakers.

- More girls than boys see themselves as friendly, happy, nice, honest, shy, or lonely.

How much freedom they have:

- Boys are more likely to be allowed to walk to school, go to a mall, or go downtown alone.

- Girls are allowed less freedom in going places on their own, and feel less safe at home and school.

TUBE TIME

Is TV a big part of kids' lives? You bet! Anne, nine, says, "TV is basically my life." From early morning cartoons to their favourite evening sitcoms, many kids are glued to the screen.

The good news is that kids don't believe everything they see. About 90% of the kids surveyed say they don't believe that TV commercials tell the truth. But kids admit they get their information about what's cool in clothes and music from television.

TIME FOR FUN

What do kids like doing best? Television and computers may take up a lot of time, but kids would rather do less of both. Kids say their number one cure for boredom is "hanging out with friends." They also like to take trips with their parents, play sports with their friends, and go camping. Many kids enjoy organized programs such as dance classes (more popular with girls) and team sports (preferred by boys). All these boredom-busters show that the thing kids find the most fun is being active with family and friends.

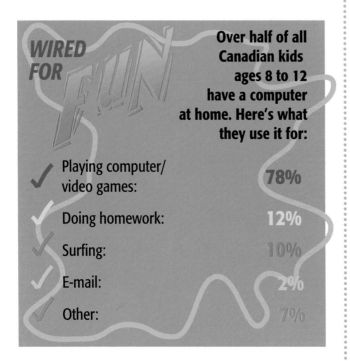

WIRED FOR FUN

Over half of all Canadian kids ages 8 to 12 have a computer at home. Here's what they use it for:

✓ Playing computer/video games: **78%**

✓ Doing homework: **12%**

✓ Surfing: 10%

✓ E-mail: 2%

✓ Other: 7%

SOURCES OF STRESS

What do kids worry about? The survey showed that number one on the list is violence at school—like bullies and teasing. "In my class, people that have just come from different countries get made fun of a lot," says Darcy, twelve.

Another big worry is success at school. Others include robbers, getting into trouble, and getting lost. Girls worry more than boys about most things, including fire, kidnapping, the environment, and even boyfriends. But more than half of all kids report feeling very safe in their neighbourhoods.

However, this survey concluded that Canadian kids are glad to be kids. "My parents say enjoy it while you can. Life's too precious to just spoil it by doing things too early," says Sophie, eleven. The researchers also found out that Canadian kids are happy to speak out about their views.

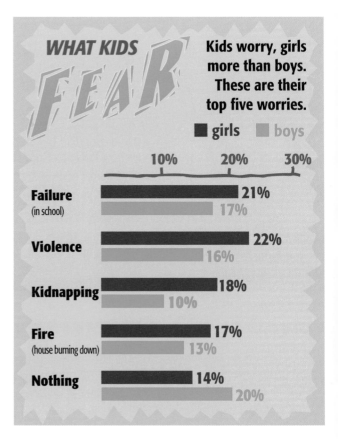

WHAT KIDS FEAR

Kids worry, girls more than boys. These are their top five worries.

■ girls ■ boys

10%	20%	30%

Failure (in school): girls **21%**, boys 17%

Violence: girls **22%**, boys 16%

Kidnapping: girls **18%**, boys 10%

Fire (house burning down): girls **17%**, boys 13%

Nothing: girls **14%**, boys **20%**

THE KIDS

For this survey, kids just like yourself, between the ages of eight and twelve, were interviewed in person and asked to complete a questionnaire. The kids come from a range of family backgrounds: two-parent homes (65%); blended two-parent families (parents have remarried) (9%); and single-parent families (23%). The researchers claim the results are 95% accurate.

How seriously should you take the conclusions found by this survey? Well, like any survey, it offers a sample of the way the average person thinks about things. Individual kids will, of course, agree or disagree with the average opinion. Surveys are never 100% accurate. But by questioning a large number of people, they can reflect the thoughts and feelings of the majority. ⬡

GROWING UP

How do Canadian kids feel about growing up? Well, most kids have mixed feelings, which means they see both a good and bad side to growing up: "I'll have more freedom," Martina, twelve, says, "but I'll have more responsibilities too."

Growing up is fun. You can explore more than you could when you were younger. You can stay up later, and try out for the basketball team.
Marie, age 11

Growing up is great because you get to go places you've never been before, learn new things, and meet new people.
Davide, age 10

Growing up is hard because there's more homework, and work at home too—washing dishes, sweeping, and taking care of my sister.
Jeff, age 12

Growing up is filled with a lot of challenges. You have decisions to make. But I know if I think positively I will get somewhere.
Diana, age 11

Do you agree or disagree with the opinions of the average kid in the survey? Which of the results surprised you? Which of the results did not surprise you?

Understanding the Article

Agree or Disagree?

Check your opinions with those in the survey!
Answer yes, no, or maybe, then explain your answer.

- Do you agree that Canadian kids are nice and honest?
- Do you think it's cool to stay in school?
- Do you agree that TV is a big part of your life?
- Are your worries similar to those in the survey?
- The survey found several differences between boys and girls. Do you agree with the findings?

Keeping a Journal

While you're working on the *Growing Up* unit, keep a personal journal. Record your thoughts about growing up, as well as your responses to the literature.

Begin your journal by recording your opinion for each question asked in the survey.

Survey Says!

Government agencies use surveys (or polls) to find out what voters think; businesses use surveys to find out what consumers might buy. Why do you think *Chatelaine* (a women's magazine) and YTV (a young people's television station) did this survey of kids' opinions? What useful information did they discover? How might they use this information? Who else might be interested in what kids are thinking about?

Design a Questionnaire

You can compare the opinions of your classmates with the survey results. Begin by picking one of the categories; for example, "Time for Fun." Write a question to be answered, and list six to ten possible answers. Add a space for "Other" in which kids can put their own ideas. For example:

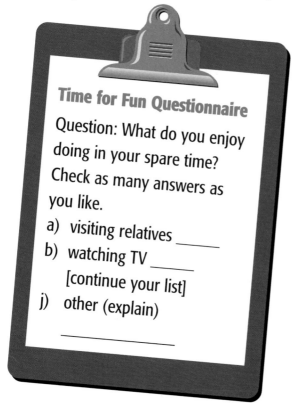

Time for Fun Questionnaire

Question: What do you enjoy doing in your spare time? Check as many answers as you like.

a) visiting relatives _____
b) watching TV _____
   [continue your list]
j) other (explain)
   _____

Make copies of your questionnaire and have your classmates fill them in. Calculate the results of your survey by following the instructions at right. Compare your classmates' opinions with the opinions of the kids surveyed in the article!

TECH LINK
Use a spreadsheet to collect and display the results of your survey.

Calculating Survey Results

Follow these instructions to calculate your survey results.

1. Count the total number of completed questionnaires.
2. Add up the number of kids who say they enjoy each activity.
3. Calculate the percentage of kids who enjoy each activity. To calculate percentage, divide the number who enjoy an activity by the total number who answered the survey, and multiply by 100. For example, if ten out of thirty kids say yes to watching TV, that equals 33%.

   $$10 \div 30 \times 100 = 33\%$$

4. Rank the activities from most enjoyed to least enjoyed (highest percentage to lowest percentage).
5. Create a chart, graph, or diagram to present your findings.

When I Grow UP

When I grow up, I think that I
may pilot rockets through the sky,
grow orchards full of apple trees,
or find a way to cure disease.
Perhaps I'll run for president,
design a robot, or invent
unique computerized machines
or miniature submarines.

When I grow up, I'd like to be
the captain of a ship at sea,
an architect, a clown or cook,
the writer of a famous book.
I just might be the one to teach
a chimpanzee the art of speech…
but what I'll *really* be, I'll bet
I've not *begun* to think of yet.

POEM BY
Jack Prelutsky

ILLUSTRATION BY
Scot Ritchie

Keeping a Journal

How many times have you been asked, "What do you want to be when you grow up?" In your journal, make a list of ten possible answers—real or funny!

POET'S CRAFT

Rhyming Couplets

Check the rhyming words in this poem, and you'll see that each pair of lines rhymes. This rhyming pattern is called "rhyming couplets," and it's often used in humorous poems.

Try writing a few rhyming couplets of your own about "growing up."

Personal Response

With your classmates, discuss the meaning of these lines:

"But what I'll *really* be, I'll bet
I've not *begun* to think of yet."

Do you ever feel this way?

BEFORE READING

Think about older relatives and friends of your family. What special knowledge do these people have? What would you most like to learn from them?

Water Spirit

Short Story by **JOEL MONTURE**   *Illustrations by* **DON KILBY**

Louis DesChamp suddenly rolled off the log he was sitting on. He was laughing so hard his stomach began to ache, and tears rolled down his brown cheeks. His father, Rene, had just put the old wood and canvas canoe in the lake by the short dock. When Rene stepped in, the bottom broke, and he fell right through the canoe. He stood up to his waist in water, holding a paddle, with a surprised look on his face.

It was springtime in Maniwaki, Québec, a land of forests, lakes, and rivers, which had been home to the Cree people for countless generations. It was also home to the majestic moose, loon, beaver, raven, and eagle. The rivers and lakes were full of trout, salmon, and bass, and it was a great thrill to go fishing after the spring thaws melted the ice on the lakes. Today, Louis was eager to go fishing, but seeing his father fall through the canoe was so funny.

"Hey, Dad," he called, regaining his voice, "catch any fish yet?"

Rene smiled and placed the paddle on the dock. "Help me get out of here."

Louis ran down and pulled on his dad's arm while Rene twisted out of the hole and climbed to the dock. "I hoped we'd get one more year out of that beat-up canoe, but I guess it's not even worth fixing now." Rene, with his short black hair and greying temples, was soaking wet. "Let's go in for a while, dry off, and think about this problem," he suggested.

They walked up a narrow path through the woods to a large log cabin in a clearing. It was a tight, warm house with a wide porch across the front under the second-story roof. Louis's mother, Margaret, sat at a table on the porch, sorting through porcupine quills that had been dyed bright colours—green, red, blue, and yellow. Beside her were rolls of thin birchbark and a basket of tools, from scissors to needles and thread. She was making little birchbark boxes with bright quill designs, which she sold in Ottawa.

She clapped a hand over her mouth to hide a wide pretty smile, then said, "What happened to you?"

"I wish you had seen it, Mom," said Louis. "Dad fell through the canoe! I'm gonna get the catalogues and look for a new one." Then he raced into the house, letting the screen door slap shut behind him.

"Hey, I didn't say anything about buying a new canoe!" called out his father.

Louis reappeared behind the screen door. "How can we go fishing without a boat?" asked Louis. "We have to buy a canoe. Maybe aluminum or fibreglass, but not some old canvas boat! I have the sporting goods catalogues in my room."

"We'll take a look," Rene agreed.

Louis raced through the house, passing his younger sister, Marie, who was colouring with crayons on the floor in the living room. "We're getting a new canoe!" he called out, jumping up the stairs to his bedroom. He rummaged around in a dresser drawer for the catalogues that had bows and hiking boots and camp stoves...and canoes!

Then he rushed downstairs toward the porch, eager to pick out a new canoe. The aluminum ones were shiny, but the fibreglass ones were bright colours, almost like his mom's porcupine quills. It would be so hard to pick out a colour— red or green or blue or yellow.

"I got the books!" he said, spreading them out on his mother's worktable. A short time later, Rene came out in dry clothing, and pulled up a folding chair. "Let's take a look," he said.

Louis thumbed through the catalogues until he came to two pages full of different canoes and prices. "I like that one a lot!" he said, pointing to a sleek red fibreglass model. "It comes in different sizes and colours, too. Some of them are six metres long," he said, reading the descriptions. "Boy, a six-metre red canoe would be great!" He looked up at his dad for approval.

Rene had a funny sparkle in his eyes. "How about that one?" he asked, pointing to the page.

Louis looked closely. The picture illustrated a white fibreglass canoe with black streaks. It was called the "Birchbark Scout, Model 200," supposedly an imitation Native canoe. "Dad, no way! It's so phony!"

"Why? What's wrong with it?"

"Birchbark canoes don't look like that. The white bark on the outside of the trees is supposed to be turned around. The brown inside bark is on the outside of a canoe, just like Mom's baskets and boxes."

"I guess they don't know what they're doing, eh?" asked Rene.

"Even I know more than they do, and I'm only twelve!" Louis wrinkled his nose.

"Brown is sort of like red, and I bet someone could make a six-metre birchbark canoe," said Louis's mother, who had been listening with a quiet smile.

Louis looked puzzled. He asked, "There are no real bark canoes in catalogues?"

"Of course not," said his father. "But we might take a drive this afternoon. What do you think, Margaret?"

"I think it would be a fine idea," she answered.

After a hearty lunch of sausages and boiled potatoes, Louis found himself riding in the family's jeep along a paved highway. They turned onto a narrow gravel road. Louis's dad was driving with his mom up front, while in the back seat Louis and his sister read books together in between watching the scenery. Marie loved it when Louis read to her, and she giggled when he made faces like the pictures of the animals.

After almost two hours of travel, they finally arrived at a small Algonquin settlement. Rene leaned out of the open car window to ask two boys carrying fishing rods, "Where is Jonas today?"

They nodded in the direction of the lake, and Rene drove a short way, parking the car near several old barns and a cabin. An old man with snowy white hair came around the corner of the barn as Rene got out of the car. Grandpa Jonas, as folks called him, squinted then grinned a big toothless smile, "*Bonjour!* Hello, Rene!" he called out.

Louis watched as his father gave the old man a strong handshake, then handed him a gift of chocolate. "Kids, Margaret, come and meet Jonas."

When Louis got out he was welcomed by Jonas, who took his hand also. His shake was very gentle when he squeezed Louis's hand, the way the old-timers did it.

"Louis, Jonas and my dad were best friends as boys. Jonas is a canoe-maker. He makes them the right way!"

Looking around the yard near the barns, Louis saw piles of wood shavings and strips of wood, big rolls of birchbark, and slabs of cedar wood leaning in the shade. Just past the yard, the lake glistened blue in the sunlight and reflected the billowy white clouds that drifted overhead. "This is a very interesting place," thought Louis.

"Jonas, you got any canoes around here?" asked Rene, winking then at Louis.

"Sure, I got some, not very big though. Come on down to the lake. I'll show you."

Louis followed close to Jonas as his family trailed behind, and when they reached the lake he saw three beautiful trim canoes resting on the stony beach. Louis ran up close to examine the skilled handiwork, from the etched designs in the bark along the gunwales to the even spruce-root stitching. His dad came beside him and said, "Maybe you want to try one out?"

Jonas leaned over and grasped the sides of the canoe, then deftly rolled it up onto his knees. Then balancing it, flipped the canoe until it rested on his shoulders. He carried it down to the water's edge and rolled it over with a splash into the lake. The canoe bobbed high on the surface of the water, and Jonas handed Louis a paddle.

"Go out. See how she handles."

Louis placed the paddle across the gunwales like his dad had taught him and maintained his balance by stepping right into the centre of the canoe, kneeling with his legs spread wide for balance. Jonas gave the canoe a shove, and it glided silently onto the lake.

This wasn't like the old canvas canoe, thought Louis, dipping his paddle with short smooth strokes. This was a fast canoe! It rocked more from side to side because it didn't have a keel. But Louis didn't tip it over. He knew how to keep his weight lowered in the boat and keep balanced by bending with his hips. When he looked back, he saw his family on the shore, waving. He spun the canoe around with several hard J-strokes, then paddled straight for shore.

"No," called Jonas. "Don't run up on the beach. Turn and come alongside."

Louis cruised in slowly and Rene grabbed the bow, helping him to step out onto the beach. "Dad, I really like this canoe!"

"You mean you don't want the red fibreglass one or the Birchbark Scout, Model 200, from the catalogue?"

"Are you crazy? This is a real canoe! Not like those bogus ones! No, I think we should buy this one!"

Rene smiled, "This one isn't for sale. And it's too small for all of us."

"Those other ones look all right," said Louis. He wanted one of Jonas's canoes so much.

"I don't think those ones are for sale either. Jonas made them for other people. One of them is going to a museum in Ottawa."

"Then what are we to do now?" asked Louis, feeling let down.

Jonas spoke up, "Lots of work to do here. Maybe you can stay with me, help me make canoes this summer. Then you can have one. Your dad says it's OK for you to learn about canoes. Maybe we can go fishing."

"Until summer we can borrow Uncle Claude's canoe," said Rene, patting Louis on the back.

Louis thought he would burst! This was even more exciting than he had dreamed. "Oh yes, I think that's a great idea. I'll work really hard, Jonas!"

As soon as school ended in June, Louis arrived to spend the summer with Jonas. In the traditional way, he referred to Jonas as Uncle, a term of friendship and respect. And Jonas sure made him work hard! Louis learned how to use a crooked knife, an old tool for shaving soft cedar wood ribs and planking used to line the bark hulls of the canoe; and he learned how to dig and pull up long pieces of spruce roots from the sandy soil, splitting them to sew the birchbark.

Sometimes they got up very early in the morning and paddled across the lake while the mist swirled on the surface of the water, hearing the whistling songs of the loons as they searched for canoe-making materials—straight cedar trees and tall thick birches. Louis enjoyed working in the forest with Jonas, because the old man often paused to point out a bird or describe a certain animal sound. Jonas also told Louis about the different plants where they worked, how some were used for medicine, some for tea, some for food by the old-timers.

One time Louis asked, "How come my dad doesn't know all this stuff?"

Jonas replied, "Oh he knows lots of this stuff, but did you ever ask him to tell you? The whole lake is full of fish, but people always think the big ones are on the other side! Sometimes you don't have to go very far to get what you want."

During the remainder of the summer, Louis became very good at stitching the bark hulls of the canoe. He even learned how to seal the seams where water would come in by covering them with pine pitch mixed with ground-up charcoal. The last step in finishing the canoes was to incise or scrape designs into the bark, which was Louis's favourite part.

By August, Louis had helped make six canoes, and one of them was for his family. It was a long canoe, with upturned ends and floral designs incised on the prows. It was big enough for his whole family to ride in, even the dog.

But the most special part of his summer was not just knowing how to make and repair birchbark canoes, it was that he and Jonas had become friends. For the rest of his life he would remember the lessons learned. When Louis and his dad went fishing together, Louis would always think of old Jonas, even years after he had passed away. When it was time for Louis to finally leave, Jonas gave him an old crooked knife with a moose antler handle. Louis reached in his pocket and gave Jonas a small beaver carved from cedar that he had made as a special gift. The old man nodded and shook the boy's hand, but this time the handshake was a little bit firmer.

Gliding silently at dawn through the lily pads the following autumn, passing ducks and loons, listening to the sounds of the natural world, Louis felt as if he were at the centre of the universe with all the water spirits around him. He had learned so much living with Jonas for a summer, and in some ways Louis had changed. He still thought fibreglass canoes were OK, but a real birchbark one was better! ●

FOLLOW UP

What does Louis learn from Jonas? Why is it important to learn lessons like these from your elders?

Understanding the Story

Great Spirit, Lifelong Friend

- What canoeing skills does Louis demonstrate the first time he goes out in Jonas's birchbark canoe?

- Why does Louis decide birchbark canoes are the best?

- What does Louis feel is the most special part of his summer with Jonas?

- In what ways has Louis changed—and grown up— over the summer?

Find Out More About...

Work with a partner to find out more about how birchbark canoes are built. Reread the story and list everything it tells you about building birchbark canoes. Then make a list of any questions you still have.

Do some research in the library and on the Internet to find an answer for each of your questions. To share your knowledge, write a how-to book about building canoes, or make a set of illustrated diagrams.

TECH LINK
Use multimedia software to present your research creatively.

Photos from *"How To Build a Birchbark Canoe"* by Tom Byers.

Story Starters

Reread the first two sentences of *Water Spirit*. How do they draw you into the story? Now read the opening sentences of some other stories and discuss with a partner why they are (or are not) effective.

Look through your writing portfolio. How could you make your opening sentences more effective? Rewrite one of your stories, changing the story starter. Ask a classmate to read your story and comment on your opening lines.

Keeping a Journal

In your journal, write a paragraph or two in response to the story. Here are a few questions to get you started:

- If you could visit Louis, what would you like to do together?
- What is special about Jonas and his relationship with Louis? Do you have a similar relationship with an older friend or family member?
- Louis's mother, Margaret, makes birchbark boxes using porcupine quills. Would you like to learn to make birchbark boxes or another craft?
- How does learning from older people help younger people become adults?

IMAGINE!

You get a hole in your shoe, your ski breaks, or your tent leaks. You don't want to buy something new, so what will you do?

Think about the things that have happened in your life recently. Have you experienced changes—good or bad? How do you feel about these changes? Whom can you talk to about them?

WHY DO THINGS HAVE TO CHANGE?

Comic Strip by **LYNN JOHNSTON**

BOY! SO YOUR MOM AN' GREG GOT MARRIED! THAT MEANS YOU'VE GOT A NEW DAD!

YEAH. ONLY THING IS... HE'S GOT TWO KIDS FROM HIS FIRST MARRIAGE.

WHAT'S WRONG WITH THAT?

MIKE, THEY'RE MOVING IN!!

ALL MY LIFE, IT'S JUST BEEN ME AN' MY MOM.

NOW, ALL OF A SUDDEN I'VE GOT A DAD AND TWO SISTERS.

EVERYONE KEEPS SAYING, "YOU'LL ADJUST, YOU'LL ADJUST...."

—WHAT AM I, A TV?

WHY IS LIFE SO COMPLICATED, MIKE? WHY DO THINGS HAFTA CHANGE?

MAYBE IT'S LIKE A VIDEO GAME! YOU GO ALONG ONE WAY, AN' THEN, BAM!—YOU GOTTA GO A DIFF'RENT WAY!

YEAH!...MAYBE WE'RE ALL A PART OF SOME HUGE, GIGANTIC GAME!

HOW DO YOU KNOW WHEN YOU'VE WON?

Do you think cartoonist Lynn Johnston knows a lot about the changes that kids go through? Why or why not?

What words would you use to describe her type of comic strip?

Understanding the Cartoon

Life Is Complicated

- Why do both Mike and Lawrence feel like strangers to each other? Do you agree that people change a lot in a year?

- Do you think Mike and Lawrence are good friends again at the end of the comic strip? What makes the difference?

- How does Lawrence feel about having a new family move in with him?

- What does Mike say to try and help Lawrence? Do you think it works?

- Why do you think people often resist or dislike changes in their lives?

Keeping a Journal

You're one of Lawrence's new sisters. Write an entry in your journal. Describe how you feel about the upcoming changes in your life, like your father marrying Lawrence's mother, and yourself getting a new brother.

CARTOONIST'S CRAFT

Drawings: Lynn Johnston's drawings show how the boys are feeling in each panel of the cartoon. What body language do they use to show these emotions: disappointment, puzzlement, resentment, hopefulness? What kinds of things are they doing while they talk?

Strips: Each strip (four boxes or panels) tells a complete story, but all the strips together tell a longer story. In each strip, the fourth panel contains the "punch line." Which is your favourite?

Dialogue: The words the characters speak are contained in dialogue balloons. Do you think the language is realistic "kidspeak"? Give some examples.

YOUR TURN TO WRITE

A Comic Strip

Create a four-panel comic strip. Invent two characters and practise drawing them doing various things. Give them a problem to worry about, then think up a humorous solution. Get your characters talking!

When you're ready, divide a long piece of paper into four panels. Make a drawing in each panel, then write the words in the dialogue balloons.

TECH LINK

Computer art programs can help you develop your comic strip.

IMAGINE!

Lawrence asks *you* why life is so complicated. You want to be helpful, of course. What is your answer?

The relationships we have with our brothers, sisters, and parents affect the way we grow up. What do you enjoy about your family relationships? What do you find difficult?

Rachel and Nathan

PROFILE BY Maxine Rosenberg   PHOTOS BY George Ancona

Rachel and her brother Nathan learned to walk at the same time. However, Rachel was ten months old when she took her first steps, and Nathan was two and a half. Nathan was born with spina bifida, a condition that paralysed him below the hips. He could not walk until he was old enough to use braces.

Like many brothers and sisters, Rachel and Nathan have common interests, mostly related to entertainment. "I teach Nathan the words to rock songs, and he tells me about the TV stars," says Rachel. "Best of all, he gives me the posters of the cute guys from his teen magazine."

They jointly put on plays for family and friends: Nathan writes the scripts and announces the shows, and Rachel sings, dances, and acts.

In the past, Rachel and Nathan weren't always so comfortable together. When they were younger, Nathan's operations, visits to doctors, and daily care occupied so much of their parents' time that Rachel often felt ignored, even on family outings. Well-meaning strangers, noticing Nathan with his braces and crutches, would approach and say, "Isn't he cute; isn't he wonderful." At those moments Rachel wished she could become invisible, to go with the way she felt.

Rachel couldn't hide, though, with Nathan around. "For years we went to the same school," she remembers. "Instead of saying, 'Hi Rachel,' kids would say, 'You're Nathan's sister, aren't you?' because he hung around me so much."

Being with Nathan constantly at school was difficult for Rachel in other ways. Rachel thought she had to protect him, even though he was older than she. When Nathan let her know that he wanted to cope on his own, things got easier. "One time some older kids challenged Nathan to a race," Rachel recalls. "I marched up to them and said, 'Leave him alone.' But Nathan told me he could handle the problem and did. In fact, when we got home, he gave me some tips on how to win an argument."

Today Rachel and Nathan go to different schools, and both have their own friends. When Rachel has a friend over, sometimes she kindly but firmly tells Nathan to disappear. "I know it takes energy for him to go find someone else to be with, but now and then I like being alone," she says. On other occasions, Nathan plays an uproarious board game with Rachel and her best friend, Kelly.

Rachel often asks Kelly to sleep over on weekends. "Kelly doesn't tease Nathan or ask him embarrassing questions," Rachel says. Rachel spends time at Kelly's house too, and sometimes goes on trips with Kelly's family.

Over the years, Rachel has learned to confide in her parents, telling them how Nathan's disability affects her. While her mother and father encourage her to do what makes her happy, they also remind her to be considerate of Nathan's condition. Sometimes the family talk together about their feelings. Before Nathan's last serious operation, they openly discussed their concerns with one another.

Rachel has also shared her feelings with a group of other children whose brothers and sisters have disabling conditions. "It was so much easier talking about problems without parents or brothers and sisters there," says Rachel. "I like doing that."

What Is Spina Bifida?

Spina bifida is a birth defect that occurs in approximately one out of every one thousand newborn babies. Spina bifida happens when a baby's spinal cord, which is formed very early in a woman's pregnancy, fails to close properly before the baby is born. Because of this gap or split in the spine, children with spina bifida are often fully, or partially, paralysed at birth. They need to learn special mobility skills, and use crutches, braces, or wheelchairs to achieve independence.

Some children with spina bifida may also have learning problems. They may have difficulty paying attention, expressing and understanding language, organizing, or learning to read and do math.

Although there is no cure for spina bifida, there are operations that can help, and research has proven that there are ways to prevent the disease from happening in the first place.

To learn more about spina bifida, contact the Spina Bifida Association of Canada at

220-338 Donald Street
Winnipeg MB R3B 2J4
1-800-565-9488

Although Rachel wishes her family could do more physical activities together, she realizes that even if her brother weren't disabled, it probably wouldn't happen. Family members don't necessarily share the same interests. Rachel's parents do not enjoy bike riding, but she likes it. Since Nathan learned to ride his specially made three-wheeler with hand pedals, the two of them go out together. "Usually Nathan wins our races because his arms are so strong," says Rachel. "But lately he's been saying he's getting too old to race with me. I hope he won't give it up—we really have fun."

Now that Rachel has so many interests of her own, she finds it hard to remember that she ever wanted to be invisible. Without much prompting, she gladly plays the piano for a willing audience or bakes a cake for a school party—"I specialize in 'gushy' ones," she jokes.

And Rachel is proud of Nathan's talents, too. She is quick to point out the ribbons he's won at horse shows, riding in the Pegasus program for people with disabilities. Also, she's first to admit that she and Nathan sometimes argue, like all brothers and sisters. "Nathan complains that I get the most attention in the family, while I say he does. It's really half and half," Rachel confesses.

"We may fight a lot now, but I know we'll be close when we're older."

FOLLOW UP

How is Rachel and Nathan's relationship like your relationships, and those of others you know? What are some of the ways that they find to solve their difficulties?

Understanding the Article

Growing Together

- When they were younger, how do you think Rachel and Nathan felt about one another?

- How did their relationship change as they grew older?

- Over the years, both Nathan and Rachel wanted to become more independent. How have they accomplished this?

- Why did communicating with their parents, and other kids, help Rachel and Nathan?

- How do you think growing up together helped both Nathan and Rachel?

Keeping a Journal

We are all different from each other in one way or another: older or younger, male or female, quiet or talkative, interested in sports or in theatre, and so on. But we have to find ways to live together—to accept and benefit from our differences.

Write a private journal entry about someone you live with who is different from you. What difficulties do you have? How do you get along? How are you working on solving your problems?

IMAGINE!

How would the article change if it were told from Nathan's point of view? Choose a story from your writing folder and try changing the point of view.

 Home Link

Create a Photo Article

The article uses both words and photos to tell a story. Sometimes the photos give details that the text doesn't. Write a caption for each photo, stating what the picture reveals about Rachel or Nathan.

Next, prepare a photo article about yourself and a family member or special friend.

Ask parents or guardians to help you find photos or take new ones. Share the first draft of your photo article with your family and friends. Use their suggestions in your final draft.

 TECH LINK

Using digital cameras or scanners can help you publish your photo article.

Something To Think About

Rachel feels that she and Nathan will be good friends when they grow up. Do you think all sisters and brothers feel this way? Do you think you will be good friends with your brother, sister, or best pal when you're all adults?

Responding Activities **37**

Yesterday

Poem by **Jean Little**

Yesterday I knew all the answers
Or I knew my parents did.

Yesterday I had my Best Friend
And my Second Best Friend
And I knew whose Best Friend I was
And who disliked me.

Yesterday I hated asparagus and coconut and parsnips
And mustard pickles and olives
And anything I'd never tasted.

Yesterday I knew what was Right and what was Wrong
And I never had any trouble deciding which was which.
It always seemed so obvious.

But today…everything's changing.
I suddenly have a million unanswered questions.
Everybody I meet might become a friend.
I tried eating snails with garlic sauce—and I liked them!
And I know the delicate shadings that lie between
Good and evil—and I face their dilemma.
Life is harder now…and yet, easier…
And more and more exciting!

Personal Response

Yesterday the speaker in the poem was very sure about things. What are some of the things she felt sure about? Did you feel more sure of things when you were younger?

Today, says the speaker, "everything's changing." She feels that she no longer has all the answers. Why is the speaker's life harder, easier, and more exciting now? Do you think this is a good description of growing up?

Trying New Food

In the poem, the speaker lists several foods she used to dislike, including things she had never tasted. But then she says she tried snails and liked them. Do you think her taste buds have changed, or her attitude? With family members, discuss the foods you (and they) used to dislike, but now like. Plan to cook and eat something new and different at your next meal!

Keeping a Journal

The poet says that she used to know what was right and what was wrong. But now she knows

"...the delicate shadings that lie between/Good and evil..."

What do you think she means?

In your journal, write some of your own thoughts on this topic. Where did you learn your ideas of right and wrong? Are you rethinking some of what you've been taught? Why?

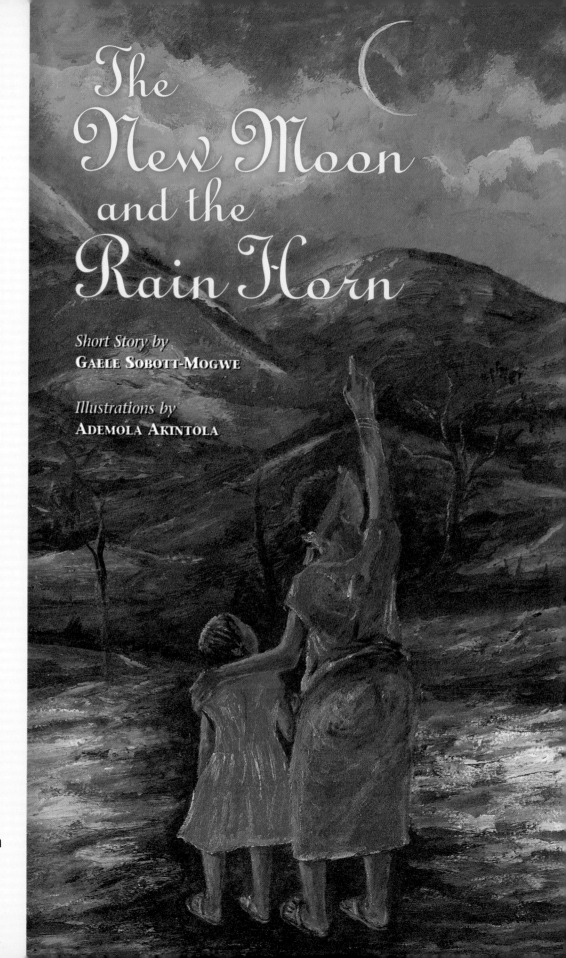

BEFORE READING

Read the first three paragraphs of the story, ending with "...the people who came before her." Make some predictions about what will happen in the story.

Will Motlalepula see the moon first one day? What will she wish for?

STORY SETTING

This story takes place in Botswana, where the author lives. You can find Botswana on a globe, on the northern border of South Africa.

Motlalepula:
mot-lah-LEE-pool-ah

The New Moon and the Rain Horn

Short Story by
GAELE SOBOTT-MOGWE

Illustrations by
ADEMOLA AKINTOLA

Motlalepula's grandmother was very, very old. When anybody asked her age, Grandmother always said, "I was born many moons ago." Motlalepula's grandmother knew time by the coming and going of the moon. She knew when it was time to plant seeds by looking at the moon, and she knew when it was time to harvest. Grandmother would say, "Motlalepula, if you are the first to see the new moon, you must make a wish. Do not make a selfish or nasty wish. Make a wish that will help the Earth and you will be happy."

But Grandmother always saw the new moon first. Sometimes Motlalepula forgot to look at the moon, and Grandmother would say, "I made my wish today." Then Motlalepula would look into the sky and see the thin slice of new moon.

Motlalepula's grandmother loved to tell stories. She told stories about how the first people came onto the Earth. She often talked about the men and women who lived in Africa before Motlalepula. She talked of old ways and she also told stories about giants and witches and wonderful animals. Motlalepula learned writing and reading and mathematics at school, but from her grandmother she learned about the Earth, the stars, and the moon, and the people who came before her.

One day, when Motlalepula was coming home from school, her grandmother called her. "Motlalepula! Put your books inside and come with me."

Motlalepula put her books in the house and followed her grandmother. Grandmother walked very slowly with the help of a walking stick that someone had given her. The handle was carved into the shape of a lion's head. There were other animal shapes cut into the stick, and Motlalepula loved looking at them. There was a rabbit, a crocodile, a monkey, an elephant, and a snake. Grandmother could walk long distances. Motlalepula often went with her after school. Grandmother showed Motlalepula different roots and plants. She taught her the names of the plants and what they could be used for.

"Look," said Grandmother, pointing to where some trees had been cut down. "People have been cutting down the trees for firewood. It is not the right time to cut down these trees and too many have been cut. These people no longer know the ways of nature. When I was young the Chief would tell the people when they could cut certain trees for firewood. Sometimes we were not to touch the trees. People do not know these things today. They will make the rain snake angry and we won't have rain. The seeds will not grow and we will not have a good harvest."

Grandmother had told Motlalepula many stories about the rain snake. The rain snake was frightening. Only people with special rainmaking power could climb the hill where the snake lived. Only people with special power could take roots and plants from the hill. The rain snake wouldn't harm rainmakers, but anyone else who dared climb the hill would disappear forever.

"Motlalepula," said Grandmother. "Today, I am going to take you to the hill where the rain snake lives."

Motlalepula thought of the giants, witches, and wonderful animals that Grandmother had spoken of. She had thought that the rain snake was just a story. Now she began to feel frightened.

"Is the rain snake real, Grandmother?"

Grandmother just laughed, and Motlalepula followed her up the hill. When they got to the top of the hill Grandmother sat on a big rock. She was tired. Motlalepula could see where they lived from the hill. She could see the village and the fields.

"When I was a child, my father taught me the secret of making rain," said Grandmother. "Now I am going to teach you that secret. I will teach you how to call soft, gentle rain that makes plants grow."

Motlalepula listened to everything her grandmother said. Grandmother opened the straw basket she had been carrying over her shoulder. Inside was a bowl and a small horn wrapped in a cloth. There were also some small bottles filled with different-coloured powders. Grandmother showed Motlalepula where to dig for roots. She picked some leaves and showed Motlalepula how to crush them into a paste. They mixed the powders and paste together in a bowl. Grandmother put some in the horn. She showed Motlalepula how to sprinkle the powder on the earth.

"When the time comes, Motlalepula, this rain horn will be yours. You must look after it. The time will come. You will know what to do."

When Grandmother died some years later, Motlalepula felt sad. She missed her grandmother very much. After school she would come home and study. She put all her energy into working for her exams. She didn't notice that the grass and trees were becoming dry and brown. She didn't notice that the crops were not growing well. There was no rain. Motlalepula still missed her grandmother, but she was too busy to think of the new moon and all that her grandmother had taught her. Motlalepula had to think about her future. She wanted to get a job. She decided to leave the village and go to the city to find work. Before Motlalepula left, her mother gave her the walking stick and straw basket that had belonged to Grandmother.

"Here, your grandmother wanted you to have these," she said gently.

Motlalepula looked into the straw basket and saw the bowl and horn wrapped in a cloth. Then she packed everything into her suitcase and set off for the city.

When she arrived she was lucky enough to find a job in the city park. She worked in the place where they grew trees and flowers from seeds. She looked after the young trees and flowers, and when they were big enough she gave them to the gardeners to plant in the park. There was plenty of water in the city, and she made sure the plants were well watered and cared for. The people in the city loved to walk under the trees and among the flowers. Motlalepula sent money home to her mother and father to help pay for her younger brother to go to school. She saved up so one day she could go to university to learn more about trees and flowers. There was a lot to do in the city, and life was busy.

One day, an old man from Motlalepula's village came to her door. "I was a friend of your grandmother's," he said. "I know that she was close to you, so I have come to ask you to help with the rain. We cannot grow anything and the animals are dying.

Motlalepula remembered the old man. She knew that he had been a good friend of her grandmother's, so she made him a cup of tea and then went into her bedroom and pulled her suitcase out from under the bed. The walking stick, the straw basket, the bowl, and the horn were inside. She had forgotten about them. She had been so busy in the city that she had not had time to think of the crops and animals. She hadn't thought of rain in the city where there was so much water. She sat there looking at the bowl and the horn for some time. She held the walking stick and looked at the animals carved on it. She thought of her grandmother and all her grandmother had taught her.

"Yes," she said to the old man. "I cannot promise to make rain, but I will try to help you."

The old man was very happy. The two of them caught a bus to the village. It was dusty and hot. When they arrived, Motlalepula left the old man and walked slowly toward the hill where the rain snake lived. She thought about the stories of the rain snake. Her grandmother had told her that only people with the power to make rain could climb the hill. Did she have the power? She was no longer frightened of the rain snake. Using her grandmother's walking stick she slowly climbed up the hill, carrying the straw basket over her shoulder. When she got to the top, Motlalepula dug up some roots and ground them into a powder. She did all the things her grandmother had taught her. She had to work quickly, as the sun was going down. When she had finished, she wrapped the horn and the bowl in the cloth and looked out across the fields and the village. As she looked, she noticed a tiny slice of silver moon in the sky. Motlalepula knew it was the new moon and she made a wish. She wished for rain.

When she came down the hill, Motlalepula walked past the place where the trees had been cut down. There was only one tree left. Motlalepula looked at the tree for a long time. Then she had an idea. She would take the seeds from this last tree to her work in the city. She would grow the seeds and look after the young trees. She picked some seed pods and wrapped them in the cloth with the horn and the bowl.

That night, as Motlalepula and her family slept, a soft, gentle rain fell. The rain continued to fall the next morning when Motlalepula caught the bus back to the city. The people of the village were very happy and Motlalepula too was happy. She looked at the seeds that she had taken from the tree. She knew that she would bring young trees back to the village. She would teach people how to plant and look after the trees like they used to when her grandmother was young, many moons ago. ◗

to **THE NEW MOON AND THE RAIN HORN**

Check the predictions you made at the beginning of the story. Were you surprised by the wish Motlalepula made? How is the setting an important part of this story?

Understanding the Story

Growing Up

- What makes Grandmother special? What secrets does she share with Motlalepula?

- Why do you think Grandmother chooses Motlalepula to carry on her work?

- Why does Motlalepula leave her village and go to the city? How does the move change her?

- What do you think is the most important lesson Grandmother teaches Motlalepula?

- What are Motlalepula's goals for her future? Do you have similar goals?

	Water Spirit	The New Moon and the Rain Horn
Younger Character		
Older Character		
Setting		
Traditional Skill Taught by Elder		
Lesson About Growing Up		

Comparing Stories

With a partner, compare *The New Moon and the Rain Horn* with the story *Water Spirit* on page 16. Make a chart like this one in your notebook and fill it in with examples from the stories.

Discuss why it is important to pass on traditional wisdom and skills to the next generation.

Keeping a Journal

What knowledge or skill would you like to learn from a grandparent, parent, or older friend? It could be the Portuguese language, the game of cricket, Ukrainian dancing, how to make a quilt—or anything at all. In your journal, write about why you would like to learn this knowledge or skill. Then ask the person to teach you. Remember, it might take months or years of study and practise, but it will be worth it!

Media Link

Something To Think About

Motlalepula's grandmother loved to tell stories, especially about the old ways of her people. Storytelling has always been an important way to teach the lessons of the past to the people of today.

What stories do your parents and grandparents tell you? Next time someone tells you a story, try taping it on a video or tape recorder. You could produce and star in your own show about families! Share your tapes with other classmates.

MORE GOOD READING

🍁 *Anywhere But Here*
by Adele Dueck
Marjorie is twelve years old, and her best friend has just moved away. She's beginning to see her life on a Saskatchewan farm in a new light.

🍁 *Cloudwalker*
by Joel Monture
If you enjoyed *Water Spirit*, you'll enjoy these other stories by Joel! In these stories he explores how six Native children preserve traditional Native ways while growing up in a modern North American society.

🍁 *The Belonging Place*
by Jean Little
This is the coming-of-age story of Elspet Mary, a young Scottish immigrant to Canada. She worries about her life in her new country, and will face loss, loneliness, and love as she searches for a place to belong.

Respect

the

Earth

Prayer for Earth

POEM BY **Myra Cohn Livingston**

Last night
an owl
called from the hill.
Coyotes howled.
A deer stood still,
nibbling at bushes far away.
The moon shone silver.
Let this stay.

Today
two noisy crows
flew by,
their shadows pasted to the sky.
The sun broke out
through clouds of grey.
An iris opened.
Let this stay.

BEFORE READING

Some people say, "One person can make a difference!" Others argue, "There's nothing one person can do to help!" Which of these statements do you think is true? Read the following two articles and think about these phrases.

Kids Who Care

Four Friends Save Sheep

Magazine Article by DOUGLAS COWELL

Every fall, when the snow begins to pile up high in the Rocky Mountains of British Columbia, a special herd of bighorn sheep move to their winter range in the valley below. It's warmer in the valley and there is less snow, so the sheep can find the grasses they like to eat.

What's special about this herd is that they spend their winter mixing with the citizens of the little town of Radium Hotsprings, situated in the southeastern part of the province. You see, the town was built right in the middle of the bighorn's winter range.

Sometimes, bighorns walking along the highway, which runs right through the community, get hit by cars. That's why four girls from Radium Hotsprings decided to do something to help the herd. Macauley Deck, Laura Frederickson, Kyla Smith, and Kelsey Verboom were classmates who formed the Rocky Mountain Bighorn Sheep Working Group.

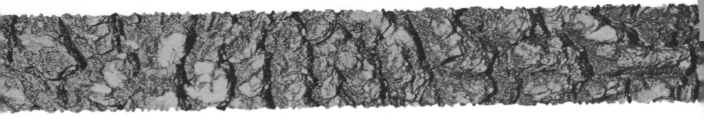

"There are tons of sheep around every winter," Macauley explains. "They walk up and down the streets, and just hang out."

The friends had noticed there were no signs posted on the highway warning motorists to watch for the sheep. "So we decided to design our own highway sign," Macauley remembers. "Laura is pretty artistic. We came up with three ideas for signs, and she drew them."

The girls showed the signs to people all over town and asked everyone to pick their favourite one. Then they took the designs and the lists of people's favourites to the town government. They convinced the mayor and town councillors to choose one design and to make signs so drivers would be more careful.

The four friends had done something important to help the sheep, and they thought their project was over. Then came the big surprise! The girls had done such a good job of teaching everyone to watch out for the sheep that the mayor and town council decided to take responsibility for protecting and helping the herd every winter.

There's even more! Now the town has decided to hold a festival every fall as the sheep come down out of the mountains. People from all over will come and celebrate these wonderful animals and help make sure they always survive.

"Kids Care...Around the World"

Schoolchildren in Finland, Denmark, Estonia, Germany, Latvia, Lithuania, Poland, Russia, and Sweden are studying pollution in the Baltic Sea, hoping to figure out ways to save the sea. Thousands of students from more than a hundred schools are involved in the Baltic Sea Project.

In Niger, children are learning how the land can be used in environmentally sound ways. They grow rice and millet in the rainy season and vegetables in the dry season.

In Indonesia, fire destroyed hundreds of hectares of forest. Local Scouts helped out by replanting trees in 480 hectares of forest.

Schoolchildren in Sweden raised money by recycling paper and cans. They used that money to buy and preserve over 60 000 hectares of rain forest in Costa Rica.

Timberrrr!

Article by Ann Love and Jane Drake

Ten years ago in January, the kids at Brockton High School in Toronto, Ontario, decided to do something about the mountain of scrap paper their school produced every week. They decided to recycle it and help save Canadian forests. The Paper Recycling Club took root. Every day their recycling team met at lunch. They picked up the school's waste paper and sorted it into bins for collection. Every two weeks, the Board of Education trucked away 160 kg of paper for recycling.

Recycling didn't make money for the school, but it saved trees. Four average-sized spruce trees are needed to make the 120 kg of paper used by every person in North America each year. Imagine how big a forest could be saved if more paper was recycled!

Preserving forests is important for wildlife. Just one tree can be home to hundreds of insects, birds, and mammals. Animals live at different levels of the forest, like dwellers in a tall tree house.

It makes sense to recycle paper and save forests, but we still need wood for houses and furniture. So some trees will continue to be cut down.

Logging companies have two choices when they plan to log a forest. They can either cut some of the trees or all of the trees. Cutting some trees is called selective logging. The trees to be cut are tagged and then carefully removed, leaving the remaining forest to grow.

The other way is clear-cut logging. Using bulldozers and chain saws, loggers cut or knock down every single tree, whether it is wanted for lumber or not. The choice trees are then hauled away and cut into planks for home building and furniture. The poorer quality wood may be left to rot or may be removed and used for products such as newspaper, cardboard boxes, or pressboard. Clear-cut logging is an easier and cheaper way to harvest trees than selective logging. That's why logging companies prefer to clear-cut forests.

There are many wildlife species, such as the pine marten, lynx, and snowshoe hare, that need a natural woodland habitat—an old-growth forest with a mixture of live trees, dead trees, and rotting trees. These habitats are threatened by clear-cut logging.

The kids at Brockton High in Toronto, Ontario, decided recycling was not enough. They held an adopt-a-tree program. Six hundred "orphan" white spruce seedlings, complete with planting instructions, were adopted by suitable families. This reforestation was free—the seedlings were donated.

Most schools around the country now recycle paper, glass, and other materials. Many schools even have compost programs for food scraps, leaves, and cut grass. Some schools have also started wildlife gardens.

FOLLOW
UP

FOLLOW
UP

After reading the articles, which statement in Before Reading do you think is true?

Have you or your friends ever noticed–or solved–problems like the ones in the articles? Tell your classmates about the problem and your solution to it.

Take *ACTION:* The Three R's

You already know about the new "three R's"–Reduce, Re-use, Recycle. But did you know that they are in that order for a reason? In a small group, talk about what these words mean, and why reducing is better than re-using, and re-using is better than recycling. How does practising the three R's help the environment? Choose one of the items below and brainstorm ideas for reducing, re-using, and recyling.

- paper at your school
- garbage at your house
- plastic bags
- shampoo and other cosmetics
- water in your home and garden
- your choice

Present your best ideas on an illustrated poster!

TECH LINK

Explore the Internet to find Web sites with stories about what kids around the world are doing to save the environment. Publish a list of these Web sites for your classmates.

Something To Think About

The authors of *Timberrrr!* say, "When we were kids we took a family trip across Vancouver Island when the huge old-growth forest was being clear-cut. We had family pictures taken on the top of an enormous stump, where the six of us could all stand. This left a lasting image, making it easier to write about the importance of forest management."

Understanding the Articles

Problem Solvers

Use point-form notes to complete a chart like this in your notebook.

	Problem	Solution	Result
Four Friends Save Sheep			
Timberrrr!			

Design a Sign

With a partner, think about a problem in your community. Do you need a safe crosswalk for children? a warning to drivers to look out for cats? a notice about a creek that floods in spring? A clear, easy-to-read sign could alert people to the problem. Choose a problem and design a sign.

1. Discuss the kind of drawing, text, and colours that make a good sign.

2. Draw a rough draft of a sign to raise awareness of your problem. Ask some friends to comment on it.

3. Paint your final sign on stiff cardboard. Post your sign in the classroom.

IMAGINE!
What can you do to help save the planet?

Summarize the Main Idea

Read the two paragraphs below about forestry techniques. For each paragraph, write one sentence summarizing the main idea. Then write one sentence that sums up the main idea of both paragraphs.

The technique of clear-cut logging, in which foresters log out every tree in an area, is becoming rare. It leaves an open, treeless plot of land that spoils the landscape. New saplings are planted, but the forest cannot be harvested again for many years.

There are good reasons to switch to a new technique called patch-cutting. Patch-cutting means removing patches of trees, leaving other trees all around. Less soil is exposed to erosion. More importantly, saplings and older trees grow back near each other. This way, foresters can continue to log the same area.

Interesting title, isn't it? Preview the photos and captions in the article. Then write down your prediction of what the title means.

PERSONAL
ACCOUNT BY
Adrian Forsyth

How Monkeys Make Chocolate

If you're ever walking through the Amazon rain forest feeling hungry, take the author's advice and follow the capuchin monkeys. They know what's delicious and what's not!

The Manu River is born in the snowy peaks of the Andes Mountains of Peru. It runs steeply downhill until it suddenly meets the Amazon rain forest. There the landscape flattens out and the river slows as it meanders through the wild and ancient forest. Gigantic fig, cedar, and kapok trees stand along the river. Some of these trees are as wide as a house at their base, and they spread a huge green canopy of leaves high in the air. But here and there the majestic scene is disturbed by a commotion.

The forests of Manu are full of monkeys. Capuchin monkeys and spider monkeys, very strong and intelligent, travel through the forest in large troops. They jump from tree to tree, crashing through the vegetation in search of food. Groups of tiny, agile squirrel monkeys often follow in their wake, swinging and chattering. They poke through the debris scattered by the larger monkeys, eating the insects their movements shake from their hiding places. There is safety in numbers—the more monkeys, the more eyes to spot predators. The squirrel monkeys get easier access to food and, without the constant need to watch for enemies, the capuchins can spend more time searching for fruit, seed pods, palm nuts, and insects to eat.

The forest of the Rio Manu is home to thousands of plants and animals, and is one of the most diverse rain forests on Earth. A brown capuchin monkey (far left) uses its keen eyes, powerful jaws, and nimble hands to find and eat a great variety of foods. Squirrel monkeys (inset above) join troops of capuchins on food-finding trips through the forest.

Cacao trees (left) grow wild in Central and South America, or are grown on plantations in tropical countries all over the world. Small midges or flies pollinate the tiny white blossoms and a few then develop into cocoa pods. Split open a pod and you will find bitter seeds surrounded by white pulp (far right).

Fruit-eating monkeys are especially eager to find one small, inconspicuous tree. As I travelled through the forest, I hardly noticed it myself, except when it sent out its strange fruits. The fruits grow right out of the trunk and branches of the tree and ripen into long, orange pods. The first time I examined a pod, I wondered what could open such a solid fruit—it was almost as big as a football and definitely too tough for most birds to eat. But it wasn't long before I saw which animals are smart and strong enough to get into the pods.

The brown capuchin monkeys were clearly excited when they found ripe pods, chattering noisily and leaping around. I watched as they pulled the pods loose and used a two-handed smash, pounding them against branches to break them open. Then they eagerly ate the contents of the pods. I did as the monkeys did and smashed a pod against a tree. The broken pod revealed several rows of seeds the size of large beans, each one coated with a glistening white coating. I took a taste, sucking the pulp off a seed. The pulp was sweet, juicy, and delicious, especially after a sweaty hike through the forest.

But the seeds inside were another matter. I broke one open and nibbled. The inside of the seed was rich brown and tasted like unsweetened cocoa powder. And that's what it is: the monkeys had found the cacao tree, and cocoa is made from its seeds. The taste of the seeds was horribly bitter after the sweet pulp, so again I followed the monkeys' actions and just spat them out as I walked along. This is how cacao trees are spread through the forest. Without monkeys to take the fruit and scatter the seeds, most of the pods would just fall into the shade of the tree and rot.

When the monkeys introduced me to the cacao tree, I was amazed at how perfectly the fruit works. The strong pod protects the seeds while they are ripening, and then it changes to a bright colour to attract monkeys when ripe. Since the pods grow right out of the trunk and branches, they are easy for monkeys to reach. The cacao tree rewards the monkey's effort with sweet pulp, a food so tasty that a monkey with a pod will tear off through the forest to keep stronger monkeys from stealing it. To make sure that the monkey eats only the pulp and spits out the seed, the seeds contain bitter chemicals (cocoa and caffeine).

The relationship between cacao and monkeys has existed for millions of years. Just a few thousand years ago, humans began to value this plant. Perhaps the first people to enjoy the fruit of the cacao discovered it the same way I did, by watching monkeys. Eventually, we learned to enjoy the strange taste inside the cocoa seeds, which we call cocoa beans because of their shape.

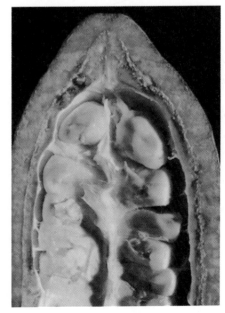

Cocoa beans are the main ingredient in chocolate, possibly the most delicious flavour humans have yet discovered. But a lot of work goes into turning the fat, bitter cocoa beans into sweet, smooth candy. Roasted cocoa beans are heated and ground into a dark paste that is called chocolate liquor, even though it doesn't contain any alcohol. Very high pressure separates the chocolate liquor into cocoa powder and a thick, golden liquid called cocoa butter. Pure chocolate candy is made from chocolate liquor, with sugar to sweeten it and extra cocoa butter to enrich it.

I once helped make chocolate from scratch. Alcides, a farmer living in west Ecuador, was tending a small patch of cacao trees near the section of rain forest where I was working. I helped him collect several bushels of yellow pods and together we piled them on the forest floor. Piling the pods seemed to heat them, which made them finish ripening. The pods were opened and the seeds spread out to dry. We roasted the dry seeds and ground them smooth, mixing them with raw brown cane sugar and a dash of cinnamon and vanilla. This mixture was heated with just enough water to make a thick paste. We rolled up the paste in aluminum foil and let it cool and harden into a solid, dark-brown roll.

Costa Rica is one of the places where people grow and process cocoa. Ripe pods can range in colour from green through yellow and orange to deep red. As the cocoa beans are removed from the pods, cleaned and dried, they turn dark brown.

Shavings of this chocolate scraped into a mug of hot water made a delicious rich-smelling drink topped with an oily layer of melted cocoa butter.

Some people drink cocoa without sugar. The Mayan people in Central America add hot pepper and drink it as a fiery, bitter brew. But most people, like monkeys, are repelled by the strong taste of cocoa beans, especially if they have just eaten the sweet pulp.

We still know very little about thousands of kinds of rain forest plants and animals. We don't even have names for many of them. But what goes on between all the plants and animals is what makes the forest work—flowers are pollinated, seeds are spread, animals are fed. Little by little, we are learning to see and to use these connections. Without the relationship between monkeys and cacao, we would not have chocolate. And living forests are full of riches yet to be found. ⬡

FOLLOW UP

●

Go back to your notebook and read your prediction. Were you right about the title? What did you find most surprising about the article?

Take ACTION: What You Can Do

In Costa Rica, the International Children's Rain Forest was saved from destruction by the children of the world. They contributed time, money, and hard work to expand and protect this sanctuary. You can help too!

- Read the book *Children Save the Rain Forest* by Dorothy Hinshaw Patent (see "More Good Books," page 89).
- Contact World Wildlife Fund for information:
    WORLD WILDLIFE FUND
    90 EGLINTON AVENUE EAST
    SUITE 501
    TORONTO ON M4P 2Z7
- Plan ways to raise money to protect rain forests.

IMAGINE!

You're a guest on a TV cooking show. The host has given you five minutes to present a history of corn (or potatoes, or strawberries, or...?) What will you say?

Understanding the Article

Monkey Business

- Explain in your own words how monkeys "make chocolate."

- How do people make chocolate from scratch?

- What message does this article send about the rain forest?

- Why do you think it's important that rain forests not be destroyed?

Contrasting Paragraphs

Reread the first two paragraphs of the article and notice the contrast. The first paragraph provides a slow, sweeping description of a "majestic scene." The second is full of noises and vivid action verbs. You can use exciting contrast in your own writing.

First, visit a natural area in your community. Take along a notebook, a field guide, a camera, and binoculars. Take photos and make notes of what you see, hear, smell, and touch. (Later, turn these notes into your first paragraph.) Next, wait for some action: small animals chasing each other, birds singing, or kids on a hike. Write down some vivid action verbs to help you describe the "commotion." (These notes will become your second paragraph.)

Polish your two paragraphs and ask a partner to read them. Make any changes that will improve your writing. Display your final version with one or two photos.

Plan a Nature Show

During the next week, watch some nature shows with your family. Discuss which show was the most exciting. What features caught your interest?

With three or four classmates, discuss what you would do to develop *How Monkeys Make Chocolate* into a nature show. What will be your opening shot? What will your narrator say? Develop a script for the show, adding technical notes about camera angles, lighting, sounds, and music. Indicate what the camera will be filming in each shot.

Create a storyboard of your TV nature show using a series of drawings. Indicate the words and sound effects to accompany each drawing.

TECH LINK
Use multimedia software to present your work.

Some Useful Media Terms and Their Meanings

voice-over: the voice of an unseen narrator

zoom shot: to move the camera quickly from a long shot to a close-up shot

fade-in: sounds or music that slowly grow in volume

fade-out: sounds or music that slowly decrease in volume

Those *Eyes*

POEM BY *Frank Asch*

ILLUSTRATION BY *Bernadette Lau*

I held you in my hands,
    heart
    beat,
    wing
    throb
And those eyes,
brighter than blood,
deeper than song,
made me believe
if only we could see
through those eyes
    nothing
    on
    this
    planet
    could
    ever
    be
    the
    same.

Personal Response

Read this poem more than once, letting images and ideas come into your mind.

- What do you think the speaker in the poem is holding?
- What does the speaker mean by seeing through "those eyes"?
- How does seeing through "those eyes" help us to respect the earth?

A Poem

In *Those Eyes,* the poet imagines what it would be like to see the world from a bird's point of view. Imagine that you are an animal— a butterfly, a whale, a turtle, a monkey. How would your point of view change? What would you be seeing, feeling, thinking?

Write a poem about this new perspective. Begin by jotting down some notes. Use *Those Eyes* as a model, or choose your own form. Take time to experiment with effective words and line lengths. Share your finished poem with a small group.

WRITER'S CRAFT
Comparisons

Reread the lines describing "those eyes":

> "brighter than blood,
>
> deeper than song"

Why did the poet choose to compare the bird's eyes to "blood" and "song"? Do these comparisons suggest that the bird is free and happy, or not?

In your notebook, complete the following comparisons. Then invent more of your own.

His hair was whiter than _____

Kallie's more fun than _____

My bike is faster than _____

Writing Tip: Next time you write, use comparisons to make your writing stronger and more interesting.

Story by
MARGARET SHAW-MACKINNON

Illustrations by
LÁSZLÓ GÁL

Tiktala

In a village in the Far North, the soapstone carvers were worried. "We are forgetting our old ways," they said, and they called a meeting.

One girl, Tiktala, waited while her mother tried to coax her father to join them. Attatak sat in silence in front of the TV, shoulders slumped, eyes dim. He had barely spoken for days. Finally, Tiktala and her mother left without him.

The meeting was long and difficult. At last, Iguptak, the wisest woman in the village, spoke, "We have many skilled soapstone carvers who sell their work for high prices. But how many of our young people care about the animal spirits that enter the stones? Who among them is willing to learn the secrets of the old carvers?"

There was silence in the room.

"I am."

Everyone turned to see who had spoken.

"I am," Tiktala said again. Tiktala wasn't like her mother who believed in spirits, and she wasn't like her father who had lost his belief in everything. She had her own reasons for wanting to carve. She wanted to be famous and admired. She wanted money to buy things—a stereo, a sewing machine, a snowmobile. Most of all, she wanted her father to notice her again. "I want to be a great carver."

"Be patient, Tiktala," one villager smiled. "Your time has not yet come."

But with her dark eyes Iguptak looked hard at Tiktala. "If you want to be a carver, you must go alone in search of a spirit helper. You must travel for three days toward the setting sun."

Tiktala was frightened, but she knew she must honour Iguptak's words. Her mother helped Tiktala prepare for the journey. When she said goodbye, Attatak raised his hand to wave, but never lifted his dark, bowed head.

For two long nights and three short days, Tiktala's feet crunched across the hardened snow. As the third night fell, she stopped, built a snow house, and lit her lamp. It was the only light in the great expanse of darkness.

In the morning, when Tiktala awoke, she was amazed to find another shelter close by. The wind blew wispy snow ghosts around it. Tiktala called into the opening. At first the only sound was a raven's cry overhead. Then, out of the opening a strange voice spoke. It was old and young, and in between, male and female, and neither.

"You have reached the place of the spirit. What is your heart's desire?"

Tiktala shivered. "I...I want to be a great carver."

"Which animal do you most want to make?"

"The harp seal," Tiktala answered without thinking. "I mean —the polar bear! The bear is greater."

"Your first choice cannot be taken back. You must go all alone to a small island in the great ocean. Time will pass for you there, but it will not pass in your village. Agree to this if you still want to carve."

"I will go," said Tiktala. "But—"

Before she could ask how to get there, Tiktala found herself on a rocky island in a vast ice-filled ocean. She was lying on the ground and felt heavy and awkward. She looked down at what should have been her mittens and saw silver-grey fur, black claws—flippers. She tried to get away, but the flippers—her flippers—scratched and scrambled on the rock. Tiktala was a harp seal.

"Spirit!" Tiktala's cry rang out. "Change me back!" But no spirit answered.

Tiktala was sick with fear. She glanced up and froze, startled, for looking at her from the icy water's edge was a dark-eyed seal like herself.

"The spirit told me you were here," said the seal quietly. "I was chosen to help you make the journey north for summer fishing. Come."

"I can't," said Tiktala. "I'm human...I was human."

"I'll try to forgive you for that," replied the seal. "But I'll tell you right now, I've suffered at human hands. I'm angry that I was chosen to help you. I told the spirit you should go by yourself, but it wouldn't listen. There is no way out for either of us."

Tiktala looked out at the black, churning waters. She dreaded the sea, but she was more afraid of being left alone. She closed her eyes and heaved forward. "I am Tiktala!" she cried, as she entered the ocean.

"And I'm Tulimak, if you even care to know. Follow me."

Tiktala felt a wave of panic as the rocky shore of the island sloped away into the shadowy depths. But when Tulimak shot downward, Tiktala followed.

As they headed north, they passed over the blue peaks of an undersea mountain range. Tulimak dove into schools of silvery fish to catch and eat. Tiktala tried to keep up, but found herself stopping to peer through shafts of light at flowing curtains of fish in the strange undersea world. Eventually, Tulimak slowed down.

"You must eat, Tiktala," she ordered sharply, "or you will not have the energy to go on."

"Why do you hate me?" asked Tiktala. "I've never done anything to you."

"Your carver spirit told me you are like the people from the old tales, who would not take a seal's life unless the seal was ready to give it. But I know better." Tulimak's face was so sad. "You are human. Humans are cruel."

Tulimak swam off and began catching fish again. Very hungry, Tiktala tried to do the same, but she wasn't quick enough.

"I see I shall have to teach you everything," snapped Tulimak. "Look. There are some herring. Just speed into the school with your mouth open—and crunch, crunch!"

By evening, Tiktala and Tulimak had chased fish from the open sea into a coastal bay.

As the Northern Lights danced above them, Tiktala asked, "Where will we sleep?"

"Here," answered Tulimak, closing her eyes right there in the bay.

Tiktala was horrified. "But Tulimak, we must go ashore! Anything could get us here. How will we breathe?" In her panic, Tiktala reached out to touch Tulimak.

Tulimak opened one sleepy eye. "Don't worry, Tiktala, I am right beside you."

Tiktala stared into the vast, dim sea and imagined things flitting about in the shadows. Finally, unable to keep her eyes open any longer, she hung vertically in the water and slept. Inch by inch Tiktala sank, gently rocked in sea dreams, until it was time to breathe. Then, still asleep, she floated up for air, and drifted downward again.

As Tiktala gained new skills on the journey, she began to enjoy Tulimak's world. And Tulimak began to accept Tiktala's company, often forgetting to be angry with her. Day after day, they swam, hunted, dozed—and sometimes even played.

Strong and graceful, with tremendous speed they travelled far, far north to the ice-filled sea, where all summer long the sun doesn't set. Such creatures they saw: huge walruses digging for clams, narwhals with their long, spiral tusks, birds diving for food, and many, many kinds of fish—cod, herring, capelin, arctic char. After what seemed to be an endless string of days, Tiktala noticed Tulimak's shape was changing.

"We'll be going south next—to the pupping ground," Tulimak told her, the old sadness back in her voice. "I'll be having a pup in a few months time."

"You should have told me," Tiktala said.

"I'm sorry, Tiktala. You are no longer my enemy, but you were human once. Don't ask too much of me."

Tiktala looked away, all at once longing for her parents. "I've had sad things in my life, too."

A new chill entered the air. Overhead, Tiktala heard the flocks of geese, the terns and swans, all of them flying south. "Time to go," said Tulimak.

One day after journeying southward, Tiktala and Tulimak lay dozing on shore ice, when a polar bear with two hungry cubs spotted them. She signalled her cubs to stay put and loped toward the seals. Quite close, she lay on her belly and waited until she was sure they were sleeping. Then she began to creep forward, hidden by the whiteness of the snow. She was so intent on getting food for her cubs that she didn't notice the wind change direction. Tulimak's nostrils twitched and she woke instantly.

Polar bear! she thought. The water was nearby. There was time to save herself. Beside her Tiktala lay asleep. So *this* was why the spirit had chosen her to guide Tiktala. Revenge. She could let this bear snatch Tiktala's life away before she was ready to give it.

Suddenly, Tulimak spotted the dark nose of the bear rising over a hump of ice. She wavered an instant and then grabbed Tiktala's flipper. "Bear!"

Tulimak dove into the sea. Tiktala followed, with the bear close behind her. Its great claws ripped her hind flipper, but she managed to plunge into the water. With their hearts pounding, the two seals never slowed until they were a long way away. At last, Tulimak swam around to look at Tiktala's torn flipper. "I'm sorry you were hurt," she said, with real sorrow. Then, unexpectedly, she was filled with joy and a new sense of freedom. She swam up, up, up, breaking the surface, soaring through sunlight.

At last they reached the great meeting place in the south where thousands of seals gather on ice to have their pups. When the moment arrived, Tulimak struggled and her pup was born—tiny, glistening, and new.

"I'd like you to name her," Tulimak told Tiktala.

Tiktala looked at the baby, a ball of soft, white fur lying there, and remembered how snow falls to earth in ever-new patterns of beauty. "I'll call her Aputi—snow on the ground," she said.

For the first time Tiktala truly yearned to be a soapstone carver. *That's what I'd carve,* she thought wistfully, *Tulimak and Aputi.*

Often, in the days that followed, Tiktala swam on her own, deep under the ice, while Tulimak fed Aputi. One morning when Tiktala came up, Tulimak was dozing alone. When Tiktala spotted Aputi, her heart almost stopped. A man was approaching her, talking softly, but holding a big wooden club in his hand. Awake now, Tulimak moaned in terror.

In that instant Tiktala knew. *This* was the human cruelty Tulimak had faced before. Aputi was not her first pup.

The man raised his weapon. Tiktala screamed and charged, desperate to place herself between the club and Aputi. As she reared up, the man disappeared and Tiktala, the girl, stood where he had been. Her arm was raised above her head, but instead of a club, she held a carving tool.

Aputi blinked up at her in surprise.

Tiktala knelt, dropping the tool on the snow. She gathered Aputi into her trembling arms and buried her face in the white, silky fur. Behind her, Tulimak barked softly in a language Tiktala no longer knew.

Tiktala stood on shaky legs and carried Aputi to her mother. She knelt and gently put her down. Aputi and Tulimak took one last look at her before slipping away, into the sea. Tiktala, tears streaming down her face, watched as the dark water closed over them.

"Now Tiktala," a voice within her said. The voice was old and young, and in between, male and female, and neither. "Now you can go home."

Tiktala found the carving tool she had dropped. She followed the bright beams of the rising sun over the purple-shadowed snow.

In three days she was home.

Before Tiktala started carving, she held the soft stone in her hands for a long, long time. Then, for hours as she worked, her spirit soared—past rocky islands, through silver curtains of fish, to a meeting place filled with the barking of seals. When she finished the carving, she smiled. She knew she didn't have to share it with anyone, but she would, for Tulimak and Aputi.

Slowly, for the first time in many days, her father looked up. A soft light filled his eyes. "You made that, Tiktala? It's yours?"

"No, Attatak," Tiktala answered, rising to place the glowing stone in his cold hands. "It is yours."

FOLLOW UP

What do you think is the most amazing part of Tiktala's adventure? How do her experiences strengthen her, her family (especially her father, Attatak), and her community?

Understanding the Story

A New Point of View

- Why is Tulimak, the seal, unwilling to help Tiktala at first? What happens to change her mind?

- What lessons does Tiktala learn about the seal's way of life?

- How does Tiktala help her father?

- What does Tiktala want at the beginning of the story? Are her desires different from yours? How? How are they the same?

- At what moment does Tiktala discover a better reason to become a carver? How has she changed by the end of the story?

IMAGINE!
How would this story have turned out if Tiktala had been granted her second wish—to be a polar bear? Write the story!

Something To Think About

Do you think Tiktala's journey was a dream? Why or why not? What truths does her journey reveal?

Many First Nations people call this kind of journey a spiritual quest. Does this phrase describe Tiktala's journey? Explain your answer.

Act It Out!

Home Link

From the story, choose an exciting scene with lots of dialogue. With one or two classmates, dramatize the scene. Read it carefully first to make sure you understand what the characters are doing and feeling. Think about how the words should be said, and what actions you will make. Prepare a script of your scene and rehearse it until you are satisfied. Then present your scene to your classmates or family members, live or on video tape.

Media Link

The Seal Hunt

In this story, we learn about the seal hunt from the point of view of Tulimak, the seal mother. What do you think the seal hunter would say about why he hunts seals?

Seal hunting is an issue that divides communities in Canada. Watch for news items on seal hunting in newspapers, on the radio, and on TV. Also look for advertisements and commercials, both for and against the seal hunt. In class, decide which point of view each media item takes: the hunters', or the environmentalists'. Discuss the difficulty of deciding what is right or wrong in such a complicated issue.

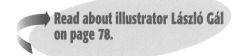

Read about illustrator László Gál on page 78.

Tiktala

László Gál

. . . .

Interview by Susan Hughes

László Gál is the illustrator of *Tiktala*. He was born in Budapest, Hungary, in 1933. He came to Canada in 1956, after the Hungarian Revolution.

Susan: Have you always been an artist?

László: I have been drawing with a pencil ever since I can remember. In Hungary, I became an art teacher. I taught for three years before I came to Canada.

Susan: When did you get a chance to illustrate your first book?

László: When I first came to Canada I washed dishes, worked as a waiter, and painted signs for restaurants. Then I got a job with the Canadian Broadcasting Corporation (CBC) as a designer. I enjoyed this work, but I began to spend my spare time painting children's illustrations. There were not many children's publishers in Canada at this time. So when my paintings were done, I took them to Italy and showed them to publishers there. One publisher commissioned me to illustrate a book. That was my beginning.

Susan: You've illustrated many books since then—and won two Governor General's awards for illustration.

László: Yes. After living in Italy for five years, I returned to Canada and continued working at the CBC. But I also kept on painting illustrations for children's books. This meant that I had to do my painting at lunchtime and in the evening. Sometimes I painted until 11:00 or 12:00 at night. Then I would get up in the morning and paint some more!

Susan: What process do you use to illustrate a picture book such as *Tiktala*?

László: First I read the story and mark the parts that I feel will make good illustrations. Then, for each of these passages, I make tiny rough pencil sketches and show them to the publisher.

Susan: What happens when these are approved?

László: I begin to do research at a library that has a large collection of photos. I find out what the characters in the book would wear, what their homes should look like, and what kind of landscape they live in.

Susan: What comes next?

László: I do full-size black-and-white line drawings of the illustrations. When they are approved, I trace them onto a white illustration board. Then I begin to use coloured pencil and paint. It takes me about a day and a half to paint one illustration.

Susan: Before illustrating *Tiktala*, had you drawn many animals?

László: No—I had drawn horses but not that many polar bears. But I enjoyed the challenge. Much of the anatomy of Arctic animals doesn't show up because of all their fur. This makes them easier to draw!

Susan: What happens to your finished paintings after the book is published?

László: I donate many of them to libraries. That way, anyone who wants to can take a look at them.

In this article, two huge oil tankers crash at sea—one off the west coast of Wales, and the other in Prince William Sound, near Alaska. Locate these places on a map or globe, and read on to find out what happened.

Oil and Water DON'T MIX

Article from WILD Magazine

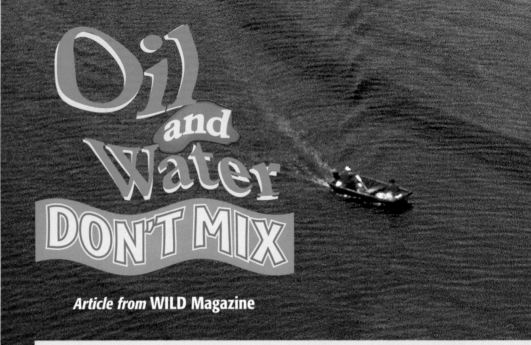

On February 15, 1995, a huge oil tanker called the *Sea Empress* sailed into some rocks off the west coast of Wales. For the next six days it was stuck there. High winds and tides battered the ship. The accident put big holes in the ship's hull and it spilled nearly 90 million litres of oil into the ocean. That's enough oil to heat 30 000 homes in Canada for one year. The storm quickly drove the oil out to sea and made it very difficult for clean-up and salvage crews to control the spill.

The crashing of the *Sea Empress* was a disaster, but it gets worse. A lot of the oil washed up on the shores of Milford Haven Estuary, a conservation area for birds and other wildlife close to where the ship crashed. This made many residents and nature lovers around the world very angry.

Oil and Water

People are upset because oil spills happen regularly. In North America, there are over 8000 spills each year. Not all of them are as big as the one caused by the *Sea Empress*. Most spills are quite small— they happen in marinas when motor boats fill up with gasoline. Bigger spills occur when oil barrels are accidentally dumped and when ships clean out their cargo holds. But no matter how much oil ends up in the water, plants and animals suffer or die.

In 1989, after an oil tanker called the *Exxon Valdez* spilled its load in Prince William Sound near Alaska, 425 000 sea birds died along with thousands of other animals, including sea otters. This ship dumped only half the oil the *Sea Empress* did! The *Exxon* spill covered 880 km of ocean and fouled about 2000 km of coastline. That's enough coastline to reach from Montréal all the way to Winnipeg.

Cleaning Up the Mess

When oil is spilled on water it forms a sheen. That's a very thin layer of oil that sits on top of and just under the water's surface. One of the jobs of clean-up crews is to try to keep the sheen from spreading out to sea. The tool they use is a containment boom. They wrap this boom around the oil spill to keep it in place. Once the oil has been contained it can be burned off the water.

Another way to get rid of the oil is to sprinkle it with a product that absorbs it, like wood waste. The waste is then scooped away before it sinks. Naturally, some oil always escapes out to sea. Eventually, the oil breaks down and forms tar balls. These balls sink to the ocean floor, then sooner or later they are washed up onto shore.

With every oil spill, some oil reaches the shoreline. The mess is unbelievable. When cleaning up a spill, the hardest job is dealing with the onshore pollution. When oil lands on rocks or mixes with sand and seaweed, it becomes really difficult to remove. Volunteers use high-pressure hoses to blast the oil with hot water. They try to push the oil back into the water. If it's in the water they can burn it or skim it off the surface.

Caring for the Animals

After an oil spill, a lot of concerned people volunteer to help care for the animals. Very little can be done to save the crustaceans, molluscs, and other small creatures that get smothered in oil. But the larger animals that are caught and cleaned can be saved.

Birds like this western grebe (right) need to have their feathers washed to survive. They're given baths with plenty of soap and are scrubbed down using toothbrushes. Turtles, otters, and all kinds of other large animals go through the same process.

Everyone's hard work pays off. Many animals are saved. But the pollution has a lasting effect—it gets into the food web and makes a lot of animals (including people) sick. Birds, fish, and scavengers like this red fox (far right) eat polluted animals and become carriers of the pollution themselves. When they get eaten by other predators, they pass it on.

Making Changes

One solution to the problem of oil spills is to build better ships. Oil tankers should be built with two hulls. This would make them safer and less likely to break apart if an accident happened.

The best way to stop oil spills is to get rid of oil altogether. But that's not so simple. Without oil, people wouldn't be able to drive their cars or motorboats, and some people wouldn't have heat for their homes. It would be impossible to live without oil right now.

But here's an idea! We could all make an effort to use less oil. Fewer cars would be on the road if we drove in car pools, used public transportation, rode our bikes, and walked more often. Instead of using motorboats (which are noisy anyway), we could canoe or sail.

Around the world, people are working on other ways to create energy. Solar power, wind power, and hydro-electric technologies are being studied and developed. So it is possible that one day we'll be able to stop using oil. And the result of that would be— no more oil spills! ⬡

What's the worst thing about oil spills in the ocean? What would you recommend as the best way to stop this ongoing problem?

Media Link

Radio News Report

With a partner, write a one-minute report for a radio news show about the crash of either the *Sea Empress* or the *Exxon Valdez.* You will need to answer the six basic reporting questions: **Who? What? When? Where? How?** and **Why?** Check library or Internet sources for more information.

Together, prepare a script for your radio report. One of you is the anchor person reading the news at the station. The other is the reporter on the scene. The anchor introduces the story, then turns it over to the reporter to give an on-the-spot account. The reporter tells what she can about the crash, quoting "eyewitnesses" to the disaster. Then the anchor asks a few questions, thanks the reporter, and concludes with a roundup of people's reactions to the disaster. "Broadcast" your final version for the class.

Understanding the Article

Disaster at Sea

- How do clean-up crews clean up oil spills on the ocean? What happens to oil that is not cleaned up?

- Why is it much harder to clean up the oil or tar on shore?

- How do volunteers clean birds and animals covered in oil? What happens if the oil is not cleaned off?

- What is a food web? How does pollution spread through a food web?

- Which of the solutions to ending oil spills do you think would be the most effective? Why?

Try an Experiment

Oil and Water

Why does oil float on water? Try this experiment to help answer this question.

You will need:
- a tall clear container
- 100 mL cold water
- 100 mL corn syrup
- 100 mL cooking oil
- a grape
- a plastic building brick
- a cork

Step 1. Pour the syrup into the container.

Step 2. Add the oil.

Step 3. Add the cold water.

Step 4. Add the cork, the plastic block, and the grape.

Observations: What happens to the oil, the water, and the syrup? Where does each item float?

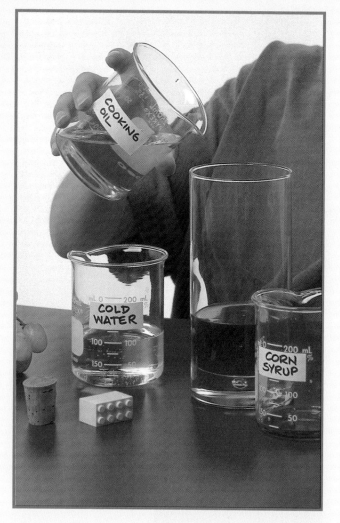

 # Keep an Energy Journal

How much energy do you use every day? That's energy for running electrical and battery-operated appliances, heating homes and water with oil or natural gas, travelling by car or public transport, and more. With your family, discuss how you all use energy, every day. How does your energy use change as the seasons change?

Here is the start of an energy journal describing how one kid uses energy. Complete your own journal, showing your own energy-using activities.

What do you know about these environmental problems: acid rain, vanishing species, holes in the ozone, polluted rivers, global warming? Read on to find out how Severn is fighting these worldwide problems.

Tell the World

Speech by **Severn Cullis-Suzuki**

Canadian student Severn Suzuki is very concerned about the environment and child poverty. One day, she spoke out about her concerns to a large audience of people from around the world. They had all come to Rio de Janeiro, Brazil, to discuss global environmental problems. Here is the speech she gave.

Hello, I'm Severn Suzuki speaking on behalf of ECO, the Environmental Children's Organization. We're a group of twelve- and thirteen-year-olds from Canada trying to make a difference. We raised all the money ourselves to come 6000 miles [over 9600 km] to tell you adults you *must* change your ways.

Coming up here today, I have no hidden agenda. I am fighting for my future. Losing my future is not like losing an election or a few points on the stock market.

I am here to speak for all future generations. I am here to speak on behalf of the starving children around the world whose cries go unheard. I am here to speak for the countless animals dying across this planet because they have nowhere left to go.

I am afraid to go out in the sun now because of the holes in the ozone. I am afraid to breathe the air because I don't know what chemicals are in it. I used to go fishing in Vancouver with my dad until just a few years ago we found the fish full of cancers. And now we hear about animals and plants becoming extinct every day—vanishing forever.

In my life, I have dreamt of seeing great herds of wild animals, jungles and rain forests full of birds and butterflies, but now I wonder if they will even exist for my children to see. Did you have to worry about these things when you were my age?

Evangelina Maya, age 18

All this is happening before our eyes and yet we act as if we have all the time we want and all the solutions. I'm only a child and I don't have all the solutions, but I want you to realize, neither do you!

You don't know how to fix the holes in our ozone layer.

You don't know how to bring salmon back to a dead stream.

You don't know how to bring back an animal now extinct.

And you can't bring back the forests that once grew where there is now a desert.

If you don't know how to fix it, please stop breaking it!

Here you may be delegates of your governments, business people, organizers, reporters, or politicians. But really you are mothers and fathers, sisters and brothers, aunts and uncles. And each of you is somebody's child.

I'm only a child yet I know we are all part of a family, five-billion strong—in fact, thirty-million species strong—and borders and governments will never change that. I'm only a child yet I know we are all in this together and should act as one single world toward one single goal. In my anger I am not blind, and in my fear I'm not afraid to tell the world how I feel.

Esther Choi, age 15

In my country we make so much waste. We buy and throw away, buy and throw away. And yet northern countries will not share with the needy. Even when we have more than enough, we are afraid to lose some of our wealth, afraid to let go.

Two days ago here in Brazil, we were shocked when we spent time with some children living on the streets. And this is what one child told us: "I wish I was rich. And if I were, I would give all the street children food, clothes, medicine, shelter, and love and affection." If a child on the street who has nothing is willing to share, why are we who have everything still so greedy?

I can't stop thinking that these children are my own age, and that it makes a tremendous difference where you are born. I could be one of those children living in the *favellas* (slums) of Rio, I could be a child starving in Somalia, a victim of war in the Middle East, or a beggar in India.

I'm only a child yet I know if all the money spent on *war* was spent on ending poverty and finding environmental answers, what a wonderful place this Earth would be.

Thank you for listening. ◈

Do you think Severn's speech impressed her audience? What do you think were the strongest points she made in the speech?

Give a Speech

Choose an environmental problem that concerns you. Collect background information about your topic. Then write a short speech that explains the problem, the causes of the problem, and how you think the problem should be solved. As you write, consider your audience: What do they already know about your subject? What are the best ways to persuade them to see your point?

When you have written your speech, memorize it. Or, learn it well enough to speak without looking down too much at your notes!

TIP > When you give your speech, speak clearly, slowly, and with feeling.

Understanding the Speech

A Young Person Speaks Out

- Who is Severn speaking for in her speech?

- What fears does she have for her future and that of other children?

- What emotions do you "hear" in her voice as you read her speech? Do you share her feelings?

- What did Severn and her friends learn by meeting street children in Brazil?

- How would you sum up the message of her speech?

Brenda Norris is a **geological engineering technologist,** who is testing the water in Baynes Sound, British Columbia.

Dr. Patrick Gregory, of the University of Victoria, is a **herpetologist** (a biologist who studies reptiles). Here he's examining a northern water snake.

David Bird is an **ornithologist** (a biologist who studies birds) who's concerned about the effect of pesticides on peregrine falcons. He works at the Raptor Research Centre in Ste-Anne-de-Bellevue, Québec.

Career Tip

ENVIRONMENTAL SCIENTIST

Environmental scientists study the effects on the environment of driving cars, operating factories, building dams, and hundreds of other actions humans engage in each day. They try to find ways to prevent damage to the land, the animals, and to people as well. If you're interested in being an environmental scientist, explore the natural areas near your home and

- visit science museums
- attend summer science camps
- get involved with environmental groups
- explore the science books in the library
- take all the science courses you can in high school
- enrol in environmental studies in university

MORE GOOD READING

Children Save the Rain Forest by Dorothy Hinshaw Patent
Beautiful colour photographs invite you to explore and learn about the Children's Rain Forest—the plants and animals that live there, why it is important, and what you can do to help preserve it. (a science book)

🍁 **The Canadian Junior Green Guide: How You Can Help Save Our World by Teri Degler and Pollution Probe**
This book includes bright and lively illustrations, clear text, and hundreds of helpful suggestions. It's a cheerful guide to saving the environment at home, at school, or on vacation. (a science activity book)

🍁 **Miracle at Willowcreek by Annette LeBox**
This story captures the beauty and mystery of a marsh. It tells the story of Tess, a young girl who loves sandhill cranes and tries to save them and their habitat. (a novel)

Peace

AND

Conflict

Fantasia

Poem by EVE MERRIAM

I dream
of
giving birth
to
a child
who will ask,
'Mother,
what was war?'

BEFORE READING

What would you do if a bully threatened you, or someone you know? Read on to discover what Ricky does in this situation.

Story by
Sigmund Brouwer

Illustrations by
Dušan Petričić

The Fight

The Bible tells the story of David, a young shepherd who defeated the fierce and murderous giant, Goliath. David defeated his huge opponent by using a slingshot. Later, David became King of what is now Israel.

Nobody past the age of two should ever be involved in a fight over a teddy bear. That's what I told myself as I began to sprint across the playground. Nobody.

But then, few people have a younger brother like Joel who insists on owning that teddy bear. And fewer are at bat during recess to notice after a big swing and miss that Randy Temples has taken the teddy bear away from Joel.

I dropped my bat and stared.

Then Randy Temples threw the teddy bear high and kicked it on its way down.

That's when I began to sprint.

Actually, there must have been a thousand times when I wanted to strangle Joel's dumb teddy bear myself, but brothers are allowed to do that. When I'm mad at Joel, I remind him that teddy bear stuffing is hard to replace. It gets his attention. But, just like all the other threats toward Joel that I mutter beneath my breath, I know deep down I'm only bluffing.

Now, to see the bewildered hurt on Joel's face, I wondered if I could ever even make that threat again. It was an expression that made me white hot angry inside. Randy Temples was big, and mean, but I guess since I was crazy enough to fight over a teddy bear, I was crazy enough not to be scared.

He saw me coming.

He held the teddy bear away from him like he dared me to grab it. What he didn't know was that by now the teddy bear was the last thing on my mind. I didn't veer half a step as I buried my head and slammed him directly in the centre of his chest.

He was as surprised as I was. We fell over together. I got up first and took the teddy bear from the ground and tossed it to Joel. Then, as my anger faded, I worried about Randy Temples.

His eyes were popping with madness. He put up his fists. I did too, not that I knew much about fighting.

"You're going to get yours, Ricky," he said.

"Just leave my brother and his bear alone," I panted.

He moved toward me. It was hard not to move back.

Then the bell rang for everyone to come in for classes.

He put his fists down. In front of everybody watching, he said, "Tonight after school you better come back here to finish this off."

I nodded.

Then he stopped and looked a little embarrassed. "I forgot. I have a doctor's appointment tonight. The fight will be tomorrow after school."

I was glad we were in different classes so that he couldn't see how nervous I was for the rest of the day.

☆ ☆ ☆ ☆ ☆

At suppertime, I couldn't eat much and my dad didn't take long to notice.

"What's up, Ricky? You're nearly as quiet as Joel tonight."

"Nothing," I said.

"Mmmph."

I would have been off the hook too, except for Joel. We had chocolate pudding with whipped cream for dessert, one of his favourites. And he didn't gobble it down with a lot of noise like usual. Instead, he took the bowl, carried it around to my side of the table, and patted my head. That meant thank you. Then he disappeared.

Dad looked at Mom.

"OK, Ricky, spill the beans," Dad said.

So I told him everything.

"You know I don't believe in fighting," he said.

"But, Dad, asking Randy Temples nicely sure wouldn't have helped. Besides, he has to know he can't pick on Joel and get away with it."

He became thoughtful. "You will need a lot of strength," he said.

"I know. Randy Temples has the biggest muscles in school."

He said something very strange. "No, son, if that kind of strength mattered, really mattered, it would be a sad world."

I just wanted advice on how to punch. I would need it.

He smiled sadly. "I'm not helping you much, am I?"

I shook my head.

Then he grinned. "OK. We'll try it my way first. Then I'll help you on yours."

Dad's way didn't seem to be much of a help. It meant a long discussion on the definition of courage, the stupidity of violence, and references to wise men and women in the past who found other solutions instead of fighting.

With that kind of attitude, I knew I'd be slaughtered after school. I looked for a way to at least be allowed one punch. I said, "Speaking of history, wouldn't you say King David was a wise man?"

Dad saw that one coming. He started to put up his hands in protest, but I pushed on.

"And didn't David kill Goliath?"

"Yes, but—" Dad tried to protest.

"Then grabbed Goliath's sword and chopped off his head?"

"Yes, but—"

"And carried the head around so everyone could see?" I quickly said. "Dripping blood and all—"

"All right, all right, all right! You made your point."

"Great," I said. "You'll give me a quick course in boxing? I promise not to chop Randy Temples' head off and—"

"I did promise you we'd try it your way, didn't I?" he interrupted. His voice then became thoughtful. "Remember this, though, Ricky, King David first had strength inside and the wisdom to know when he really had to fight."

Then his face lit up in a grin. "Now, let's discuss how we'll do it your way if it becomes necessary."

☆ ☆ ☆ ☆ ☆

Naturally, everybody at school knew about the upcoming fight between me and Randy Temples after school.

Mike asked me if he could have my comic books while I was in the hospital. Questions like that don't help your frame of mind.

Before I knew it, school was over for the day. I walked slowly over to the baseball diamond. Randy Temples was there with a mean look on his face. All his friends and all my friends were there; so was nearly everyone else.

He took off his jacket. So did I. I had on my heaviest and loosest sweater.

He put up his fists.

I didn't.

"Fight," he said.

I shook my head. "I want you to leave my brother alone. And I think fighting is a dumb way to do this."

He sneered and his friends laughed. "You're chicken," he said. "I knew it."

"No, I'm not chicken." I tried the logic that my dad had used on me. "Fighting only proves one of us is a better fighter than the other, and just because you're a better fighter doesn't mean you're right."

With everyone watching, it was still pretty quiet.

"Nice try, chicken." To his friends, he said, "Let's go, guys. I can't stand cowards."

"Stay," I said. "Nobody here is a coward." I pointed to my stomach. "Hit me."

"What?"

"Hit me. If you think you are proving something by fighting, go ahead. Hit me. I'm not scared of you. I just won't fight back."

He grinned. "Great. Watch this, guys. I'll hit him so hard he'll get picked up for speeding."

He moved real close to me. His breathing was heavy.

I put my hands on my hips to give him my whole stomach to punch.

Over his shoulder he said, "I'll hit him so hard, he'll fall into tomorrow."

He brought his fist back to swing. I tried not to flinch.

Then he swung. I didn't move to protect myself.

Nothing happened. He had missed on purpose.

There was disbelief on his face that I would just let him take his hardest swing at me.

"You mean it, don't you," he said. "You won't run away, but you won't fight back. Are you crazy?"

"No," I said. "I think I'm right, though. That makes it easier."

He brought his fist back again and studied my face. I was prepared to let him swing.

"Ah, forget it," he said. "I don't care if your dumb brother marries that teddy bear."

After that, he didn't bother me or Joel much. In fact, he even became my friend later. But I never told him how badly he would have hurt himself by swinging that day.

Because when I got home that night, Dad asked, "Did you learn something about the strength of courage today?"

I nodded. "He didn't hit me."

Dad said, "Good. It's a tough lesson. I hope you can remember it when you need to show wisdom again." He grinned. "Next time you might not be wearing your backup plan."

I grinned back and took off my loose and bulky sweater.

Dad helped me remove the backup plan that I wore underneath. It was a square piece of board that we had strapped for protection across my stomach in the morning before I went to school. After all, as Dad had reminded me, King David used the smartest way possible whenever he actually had to fight. ●

Is Ricky's way of dealing with Randy, the bully, anything like your approach? What would you have done differently?

Understanding the Story

Peace Options

- What do you think of the advice Ricky gets from his dad?

- Why does Ricky bring up the biblical story of David and Goliath? What message does his father take from the story?

- Why is Randy scornful when Ricky refuses to fight?

- How do the boys end up solving their conflict? Do you think either of them really wanted to fight? Explain your answer.

IMAGINE!

For one week, everyone in the world refuses to fight. What would it be like?

Advice from Grown-Ups

Take the story home and read it to your mother, father, or guardian. Ask them if they agree with the advice Ricky's father gives him. If you were facing a possible fight, what solution would they suggest to you?

Conflict Resolution

GROUP DISCUSSION

Many schools have a policy of "No Violence!" and students must solve their problems without fighting. Choose one of the conflict situations in the list below. Discuss how you could solve the problem without using violence. Present your solutions to the class.

- an older student is forcing a younger student to hand over his lunch

- a bully and her pals are making it impossible for other children to use the playground after school

- a few students are picking on another student who is of a different race or colour

- a situation of your choice

TECH LINK

Post your ideas for solving conflicts on the school's Web site.

YOUR TURN TO WRITE

A Story

Author Sigmund Brouwer uses a couple of good techniques to keep the reader interested: **suspense** and a **surprise ending.** Suspense means keeping the reader on edge, wondering what's going to happen next—especially in a scary action story. A surprise ending means just what it says. In *The Fight*, the author reveals at the very last minute that Ricky is wearing a secret shield.

Write your own story about a fight. It may be based on experience, or on stories you have read or seen on television. Give it some suspense, and maybe a surprise ending, too!

BEFORE READING

How to stop people from fighting has been a problem throughout the ages. In these traditional folk tales, conflict is resolved in two interesting ways.

Folk tales and Proverbs collected by
Margaret Read MacDonald

Illustrations by
Jackie Besteman

Tales

The Argument Sticks

Two boys were arguing. Neither would admit he was wrong. They were about to come to blows over this.

Their mother gave them three sticks: "These are special Argument Sticks. They will solve this argument for you. Set your sticks up in the woods, leaning one against the other so they all stand up. Leave them there for one month. If they fall over toward the north, the one who sets up the northern stick is right in this matter. If they fall over toward the south, the one who sets up the southern stick is right in this matter."

The boys took their sticks into the woods and set them up. They were satisfied that this would solve their argument. A month later the boys remembered their Argument Sticks. They went into the woods to find out who had won the argument.

The sticks had fallen in a heap and begun to rot. There was no winner.

And the boys couldn't remember what the argument had been about in the first place.

—An Iroquois Tale

Equality breeds no war.
Gleich und gleich fängt keinen Krieg an.
—A German Proverb

One thousand friends are too little; one enemy is too many.
Dost bin ise azdir; düsman bir ise çoktur.
—A Turkish Proverb

for Peace

Two Goats on the Bridge

Between two mountains lay a narrow bridge. On each mountain lived a goat. Some days the goat from the western mountain would cross the bridge to graze on the eastern mountain. Some days the goat from the eastern mountain would cross the bridge to graze on the western mountain. But one day both goats began to cross the bridge at the same time.

The two goats met in the middle of the bridge.

"We have a problem here," said the Western Goat.

"So it seems," said the Eastern Goat.

"I do not want to back up," said the Western Goat.

"Neither do I," said the Eastern Goat. "This bridge is narrow, but perhaps…"

"Perhaps if we both are very careful…" added the Western Goat.

"…We could pass without FALLING!" concluded the Eastern Goat.

"We can TRY," agreed the two goats.

And cautiously they squeezed past, each being careful not to overbalance the other.

Thus the goats passed peacefully and went on their way. Each could be heard to mutter, "What a co-operative fellow he is!"

—A Tale from Eastern Europe

It is well to be united in thought, that all have peace.
E waikahi ka pono i manalo.
—A Hawaiian Proverb

Convert great quarrels into small ones, and small ones into nothing.
Ta shih hua hsiao, hsiao shih hua wu.
—A Chinese Proverb

When there is no one against you, you cannot quarrel.
Aite no nai kenka wa dekinu.
—A Japenese Proverb

Respect for the rights of another, that is peace.
El respeto al derecho ajeno es la paz.
—A Mexican-American Proverb

103

**FOLLOW
UP**

Which of the two tales is your favourite? Do you think the tales have good lessons to teach people today?

Understanding the Tales

Lessons of Peace

- What lessons can be learned from both these tales?
- Do you think the stick trick would work a second time, once people had heard about it?
- Could the goats' solution work over and over again in different situations? Explain why, or why not.
- What messages do the proverbs contain?
- What do these proverbs remind you of?

IMAGINE!

Two goats meet in the middle of a narrow bridge. Each of the goats refuses to compromise. What happens next?

Create a Puppet Show

Either of these tales could be turned into a puppet show for younger children. In a small group, design and build the puppets. Decide how the puppets should look and how you will make them move. Be inventive! Choose a narrator to read the tales, and actors to learn the speeches in quotation marks.

TIP > Both tales make their points in a humorous fashion. Think of actions and gestures that will get your young audience laughing.

Retelling Tales

ORAL LANGUAGE

Work with a partner to retell one of the peace tales. Practise reading one of the tales out loud so that you bring out both the humour and the lesson the tale is teaching. When you know the tale very well, retell it to a small group without reading it. You can use your own words: there's no need to stick to the original text when you're retelling a story!

YOUR TURN TO WRITE

A Peace Tale

These short tales are clever and fun to read. They're fun to write, too! Below are some ideas to get you started on writing your own peace tale with a lesson. Be sure to use lots of dialogue in your tale.

- a musician is attacked by pirates
- two friends are competing for one place on a team
- a family of mice vow to get revenge on a cat
- islanders want to stop the building of a bridge to their island

BEFORE READING

In this story, Zada, a girl from Baghdad, writes to Margaret, her American friend. Zada is anxiously expecting American bombs to hit her city.

On a map of the world, find Baghdad (the capital city of Iraq) and the neighbouring country of Kuwait.

Letter Story by
Barbara Bedway

Illustrations by
Jack McMaster

Letters from Baghdad

January 5

Dear Margaret,

It seems a million years ago that we got your Christmas card. Mother and I pray every day that we will not have war. Margaret, please pray too.

Everyone is buying as much food as they can. The basement of our house—do you remember how we liked to play cards there because it was cool and eat pistachio nuts out of a sack on the floor?—well, now it's full of barrels holding pistachios and raisins and wheat, and the freezer is full to bursting with lamb and chickens. You could fall over the stacks of toilet paper and tea and spaghetti. Everyone's put masking tape on the windows, for when the bombs come. Do you think it will really happen?

(over →)

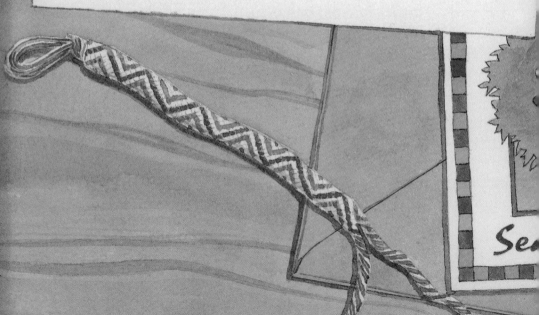

Mother had a good idea for how I can keep up my English. We speak Arabic downstairs, and only English upstairs. It's fun, because I remember how you and I would sit on my bed and brush each other's hair and talk about clothes and boys and music. I still remember all the words to Paula Abdul's "Forever Your Girl." Sometimes I pretend it's you I am talking to upstairs, though Adnan makes fun of me.

Are you keeping up with your Arabic? Remember how Adnan taught you to say *Mish melleh*, "No problem," whenever you were asked something and you didn't understand? Sometimes, when the news is scary and the house looks so gloomy with windows taped shut, I think about your visit last summer and wonder if I will ever get to visit you in America. I would like to be an archaeologist like your father when I grow up, and travel all over the world like he does. Mother says my father wanted to travel the wide world too, but he only got as far as Iran before he died.

Sincerely yours,
Zada

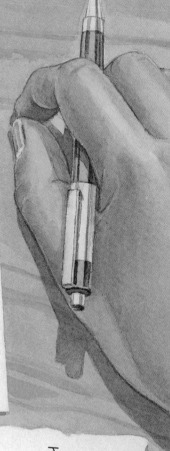

's Greetings

Dear Margaret,

January 10

Adnan was called up for military registration today. We drove him in a cold rain to the military barracks. A friend in the ministry is trying to get him a deferment, but we do not have that much money. On the way there, the car radio played love songs, the mushy kind you made fun of when you were here. But now the radio plays only military songs, songs about fighting and dying for our country, and I wish we could hear the love again.

Sincerely,
Zada

Dear Margaret,   January 12

Can you be getting my letters? I have no way to know.
We've moved to the Al Rashid Hotel, where Mother is
working as a translator for one of the television
reporters. We sleep in the lobby to be close to the
bomb shelter in the basement. It is too late to escape,
Mother says. The airport is closed, we can't find gas
for our car. But she is certain the United States will not
bomb this hotel, because there are so many Americans
and Europeans here. Everyone talks about the bombs.
Some people say there are special bombs that crash
through all the stories of the building and then explode.
Margaret, will you tell your president about us, that we
are here?

                    Yours truly,
                    Zada

                                                           January 16

Dear Margaret,

I know you may not ever receive these letters, at least
not for a long time. Still I write them, because a reporter
from America promised to take them when he leaves. I
wish he would take us, too.
    The war came at 2:35 this morning. I know the time
because I never take off the watch you gave me. It is my
lucky charm. The whole city is blacked out at night, but the
bombs found us anyway. We heard the boom and thud and
saw one red ball high in the black sky before it exploded
and we were all rushing for the basement stairs. The
explosions fill up your ears and make my mother shake.
But I don't shake; I stay as still as possible. I was the one
who spread out our blanket and told my mother to lie down.
All around us other families lie curled up on their blankets,
too. It's like a giant slumber party, only no one talks much
and everyone is afraid.

                    Sincerely,
                    Zada

February 1

Dear Margaret,

That reporter I told you about is leaving today for Jordan, and then back to America. This might be the last letter I can hope to get to you for a long time. People fill the hotel hallways dragging their suitcases, and I wish we could go away too, but we cannot leave without knowing the fate of my brother. He is somewhere on active duty. Mother says that maybe because Adnan speaks good English Saddam will save him for the peace. We pray for this.

Sincerely yours,
Zada

April 10

Dear Margaret,

The miracles I want are peace and my brother safe and a letter from you. Things are getting a little better here. We are out of the hotel and back home. Our whole street has electricity again, and sometimes the telephones work. There is food in the stores, but everything costs so much money. We are not starving, but we are all hungry. Does the world hate us now? Sometimes I feel as though I am living at the end of the world. Please, please write soon.

Sincerely yours,
Zada

May 25

Dear Margaret,

Your letter from months ago arrived at last. I read it to Adnan in the hospital and I think that was a smile, underneath his bandages. He has lost one eye and the fingers of his right hand. We know that he is lucky, lucky to be alive, but still my mother cries over him when she visits. He likes me to sing the songs you taught me, "Forever Your Girl" and "Everlasting Love" and "If You Don't Know Me By Now." We will take him home soon because the hospital needs the space for others, and they are running out of his medicine, too. If you ask Adnan how we will find more medicine, or pay for food, you can guess what his answer will be *Mish melleh*, he says, but I know better now.

Truly yours,
Zada

How do you think
Zada and Margaret
feel about the war?
How would you feel
if your country
went to war against
the country where a
friend of yours was
living?

YOUR TURN
TO WRITE

A Letter to a Friend

In the selection, we don't read the letter that
Zada finally received from Margaret. What do
you think that letter said? Remember, it was
written "months ago." Write that letter, or any
other letter that Margaret might have sent to
her friend in Iraq. Include lots of news and
lots of questions!

IMAGINE!

Margaret introduces Zada to her favourite popular
songs. What songs would you teach
a friend in another country?

Something To Think About

**Nobody knows exactly
how many Iraqi civilians were
killed during the Gulf War, but
it was probably thousands.**

**Why would one country
declare war on another?
Of course, the reasons both
sides would give are very
complicated. Do you think
war is ever a good solution?
Explain your answer.**

Understanding the Selection

- How do you think Zada and Margaret became
  friends?
- Why do Zada and her mother stock up on food?
- Why do they move to the Al Rashid Hotel?
- After the bombing stops and Adnan comes home,
  what does Zada worry about?

Take *ACTION!*

The United Nations Children's Fund (UNICEF) reports that during most conflicts, children are the greatest victims. There are things we can all do to achieve peace, and protect children. For example, twenty-two students (below) from Ancaster Public School in Toronto, Ontario, presented their Bill of Rights to an international conference on land mines. This Bill of Rights listed how children around the world should be protected from land mines. (right)

With your classmates, plan an anti-violence activity day for your school. Have fun, and make peace a part of your lives.

Bill of Rights

Children, being the innocent victims of land mines, have a right to the following:

- To recognize the appearance of land mines and to learn about them.
- To know where land mines are.
- To live and play in land mine-free areas.
- To live with dignity and respect if hurt by land mines.
- To the best possible medical care at no cost to their families if damaged by a land mine.
- To be supervised.
- To go to school, even if they have been hurt by land mines.
- To signs, posted in a form which they can understand, warning them of land mine danger.
- To expect that land mines will be removed from their communities.

Fulfilling these rights is the responsibility of the world community.

The Paint-Box

Poem by Tali Shurek (Be'er Sheva, Israel)

I had a paint-box—
Each colour glowing with delight;
I had a paint-box with colours
Warm and cool and bright.
I had no red for wounds and blood,
I had no black for an orphaned child,
I had no white for the face of the dead,
I had no yellow for burning sands.
I had orange for joy and life,
I had green for buds and blooms,
I had blue for clear bright skies,
I had pink for dreams and rest.
I sat down
and painted
Peace.

War Is Here

Poem by Students (Zenica, Bosnia-Hercegovina)

War is here, but we await peace. We are in a corner of the world where nobody seems to hear us. But we are not afraid, and we will not give up.

Our parents earn little, just barely enough to buy five kilos of flour a month. And we have no water, no electricity, no heat. We bear it all, but we cannot bear the hate and the evil.

Our teacher has told us about Anne Frank, and we have read her diary. After fifty years, history is repeating itself right here with this war, with the hate and the killing, and with having to hide to save your life.

We are only twelve years old. We can't influence politics and the war, but we want to live! And we want to stop this madness. Like Anne Frank fifty years ago, we wait for peace. She didn't live to see it. Will we?

Personal Response

In these two poems, real children who have lived through war cry out for peace. What would you like to say to the students in Zenica? What kinds of experiences do you think Tali Shurek has lived through?

You are the Artist

Using Tali Shurek's choice of colours, make a painting of **peace**. Let your imagination run away with you!

The Story of *In Flanders Fields*

Preview this selection by looking at the illustrations, the poem, and the subheadings in the article. What do you think you will learn from your reading?

In Flanders Fields

In Flanders fields the poppies blow
Between the crosses, row on row,
That mark our place; and in the sky
The larks, still bravely singing, fly
Scarce heard amid the guns below.

We are the Dead. Short days ago
We lived, felt dawn, saw sunset glow,
Loved, and were loved, and now we lie
    In Flanders fields.

Take up our quarrel with the foe:
To you from failing hands we throw
    The torch; be yours to hold it high.
If ye break faith with us who die
We shall not sleep, though poppies grow
    In Flanders fields.

Poem by
JOHN MCCRAE

Historical
Account by
LINDA GRANFIELD

Illustrations by
JANET WILSON

114

A Poem Written on a Battlefield

The story of *In Flanders Fields* begins in May 1915, in Flanders—French and Belgian lands bordered by the North Sea. It was time for the fresh green shoots and white blossoms to appear. But the First World War had raged for nearly a year and winter's gloom remained, etched upon the skies by blackened tree trunks, ruined church spires, and barbed wire.

For nearly two weeks John McCrae, a Canadian medical officer, had tended the horrible injuries suffered by soldiers in the Second Battle of Ypres. While shells exploded around them, McCrae and his staff cared for hundreds of wounded soldiers each day. And others, companions they had shared a meal with just hours before, were buried a few steps from the dressing-station* door. McCrae later wrote, "We really expected to die in our tracks. We never had our boots off, much less our clothes."

On the second dismal day of May, one death in particular touched John McCrae. A close friend, Lieutenant Alexis Helmer, was killed early that morning when an enemy shell exploded at his feet. John McCrae, doctor, could do nothing to save him. But John McCrae, soldier and friend, recited prayers as Helmer's remains were lowered into the Flanders soil and the grave marked with a wooden cross.

---

* **dressing station:** a centre that gives first aid to wounded soldiers. It is located close to the combat area.

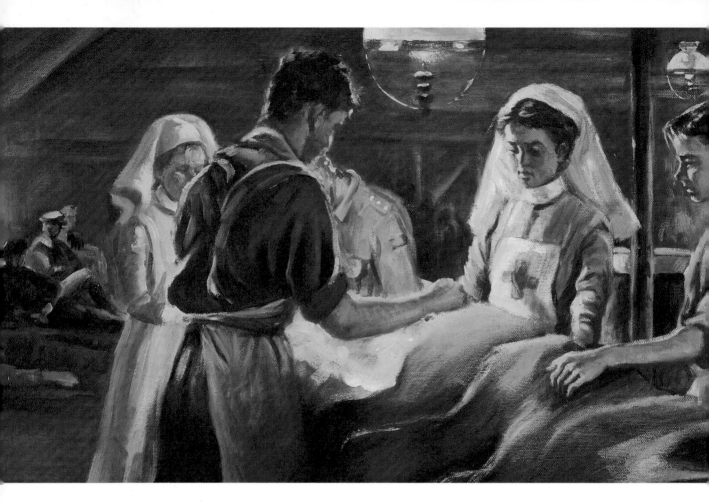

Reports concerning the hours after Helmer's burial differ. One states that McCrae sat on the back step of an ambulance, writing within sight of the new grave. Another says the doctor wrote off and on while bandaging the wounded. *What* he was writing, however, proved more important than *where* he wrote it. Helmer's death inspired McCrae to write *In Flanders Fields*, a poem that to this day relays the images of war, loss, love, and renewal.

After he completed the poem, John McCrae was back at work in the dressing station. The war was to continue for three more years in Flanders fields and beyond.

A Canadian Doctor Goes to War

The First World War began in August 1914, when Germany invaded Belgium. This caused Britain and its Allies* to declare

---

* **Allies:** those countries—Britain, France, Italy, Portugal, Russia, Canada, China, Japan, and many others—that formed an alliance to fight against Germany and Austria-Hungary in the First World War.

war on Germany. The Great War, as it was called, was unlike any other in history. It was a new and horrible artillery battle fought from rat-infested, water-filled trenches dug deep into foreign soil. There was little noble about it, except the dedication of millions to fight for what they believed. Into the nightmarish terrain of the Western Front stepped John McCrae.

McCrae's ancestors included soldiers and physicians, and he carried on both traditions. As a boy in Guelph, Ontario, he won a gold medal for being the best drilled cadet in the province. By fifteen he was a bugler in his father's battery, and by eighteen he was a gunner. While in university, McCrae belonged to the Queen's Own Rifles. Medical school was followed by American and Canadian hospital work and teaching. All the while, McCrae wrote short stories and poetry in which peace after death was a repeated theme.

The battlefields of Flanders were not the first John McCrae had ever encountered. In 1900, he sailed from Halifax, Nova Scotia, to South Africa, where the Boer War was blazing. There he saw first-hand the cost of battle, though still he believed that a person must fight evil wherever it occurred. After a year in South Africa, McCrae returned to Canada, and for ten years he was a doctor and a teacher, not a soldier.

McCrae was in England on holiday when war was declared in 1914, yet he answered Canada's call for recruits. "I'm available as a combatant or medical if they need me," he cabled home.

But after a year in Flanders, McCrae wrote to a close friend, "I saw enough fighting to do me for my natural life." Millions of others from many nations no doubt agreed.

The Most Popular Poem of the Great War

Soon after he wrote *In Flanders Fields*, John McCrae sent the poem to England for possible publication. It appeared, without his name, in the December 8, 1915, issue of *Punch* magazine. The public response was overwhelming. The poet's identity was subsequently revealed, and his work became known as "the most popular English poem of the Great War." In just fifteen lines, McCrae had captured the mood of the times.

The United States entered the War in 1917, and the fighting continued. Countries were ruined, and people and resources were exhausted. Some officials thought the war might go on until 1920, but improved tanks, airplanes, and renewed military strategies brought it to a gradual end. In the early morning hours of November 11, 1918, the Armistice, an agreement to end the fighting, was signed. By the eleventh hour of the eleventh day of the eleventh month, after nearly sixteen hundred days of war, the guns were silenced.

Millions had been killed and thousands more returned home with permanently damaged bodies. Few people were left untouched by the horrors of the battlefield.

Memorials began to dot the countrysides of many nations, "lest we forget." Now every November 11 at 11 a.m., silence descends on streets everywhere as millions of people pause to reflect on the enormous losses sustained by the world during wartime. To this day, *In Flanders Fields* is recited during remembrance ceremonies around the world.

Some people argue that the poem's invitation to battle is unsettling. Others recognize it as an expression of John McCrae's personal beliefs and an example of social attitudes of the time. While almost everyone can agree that war has never erased the problems of the world, we continue to honour the memory of those who sacrificed themselves for a cause they believed to be great and just. Often, voices of peace, like McCrae's larks, may *scarce* be heard, but they *can* be heard...if only we will listen. ⬡

Postscript: Sadly, Dr. John McCrae died of pneumonia on January 28, 1918—before the war ended. But his voice can still be heard long after his death.

FOLLOW UP

What did you learn about John McCrae, the war he fought in, and the famous poem he wrote? Write down three questions you still have.

Understanding the Poem

Voices From Our Past

- Who is speaking in the poem? Who is meant to be listening?
- In verse one, the bright lively poppies are contrasted with the quiet rows of crosses marking the graves. What are the singing larks contrasted with?
- Verse two points out another sad contrast. What is it?
- What is the message sent by the Dead in verse three? In your opinion, is it a message of war, or of peace?

Understanding the Article

The Life of a Hero

- What event inspired Dr. John McCrae to write the poem *In Flanders Fields*?
- Based on his life story, why does it make sense that McCrae volunteered to go to war in 1914?
- Why do you think his poem was so popular when it was published in 1915?
- Do you agree that "the poem's invitation to battle is unsettling"? If not, how do you feel about the message of the poem?

Words in Time of War

Reread the text to find these words:

artillery   combatant

trenches   bridge

Figure out what each word means by how it is used in the sentence. Write your own definition. Check a dictionary to see if your definitions are correct, and to find out how the words are pronounced.

"If ye break faith — we shall not sleep"

Something To Think About

John McCrae feels that it is right to go to war and fight for what you believe in— if the cause is "great and just." Pacifists, on the other hand, believe that war is always wrong; they refuse to fight for any reason. What do you think about these two positions?

Design a Poster

Think of a message that you would like to convey for Remembrance Day on November 11. Select words that express your message, then experiment with styles and sizes of type. Leave lots of room to draw or paint an effective image. Choose colours that will attract attention to your poster.

TECH LINK
Experiment with different types and sizes of letters on a computer word-processing program.

Choral Reading

Since *In Flanders Fields* has more than one speaker, it would be effective to have a group of readers perform it. With your group, decide who will read each verse. What feelings does each verse bring out? How will you convey these emotions with voices and gestures?

Sadako Sasaki was a real Japanese girl living in Hiroshima when the atom bomb dropped on that city in 1945. This story tells about her life and the powerful effect she has had on young people everywhere.

Sadako

STORY BY *Eleanor Coerr*   PAINTINGS BY *Ed Young*

Japanese Words

obasan: grandmother

chan: added to a child's name, it means "dear little…"

Kokeshi doll: a painted wooden doll

One morning in August 1954, Sadako Sasaki looked up at the blue sky over Hiroshima and saw not a cloud in the sky. It was a good sign. Sadako was always looking for good-luck signs.

Back in the house, her sister and brothers were still sleeping on their bed quilts. She poked her big brother, Masahiro.

"Get up, lazybones!" she said. "It's Peace Day!"

Masahiro groaned, but when he sniffed the good smell of bean soup, he got up. Soon Mitsue and Eiji were awake, too.

Rushing like a whirlwind into the kitchen, Sadako cried, "Mother can we please hurry with breakfast? I can hardly wait for the carnival!"

"You must not call it a carnival," her mother said. "It is a memorial day for those who died when the atom bomb was dropped on our city. Your own grandmother was killed, and you must show respect."

"But I do respect Obasan," Sadako said. "It's just that I feel so happy today."

At breakfast, Sadako fidgeted and wriggled her bare toes. Her thoughts were dancing around the Peace Day of last year—the crowds, the music, and the fireworks. She could almost taste the spun cotton candy.

She jumped up when there was a knock at the door. It was Chizuko, her best friend. The two were as close as two pine needles on the same twig.

"Mother, may we go ahead to the Peace Park?" Sadako asked.

"Yes, Sadako chan," her mother answered. "Go slowly in this heat!" But the two girls were already racing up the dusty street.

Mr. Sasaki laughed. "Did you ever see Sadako walk when she could run, hop, or jump?"

At the entrance to the Peace Park, people filed through the memorial building in silence. On the walls were photographs of the ruined city after the atom bomb—the Thunderbolt—had instantly turned Hiroshima into a desert.

"I remember the Thunderbolt," Sadako whispered. "There was the flash of a million suns. Then the heat prickled my eyes like needles."

"How could you possibly remember anything?" Chizuko exclaimed. "You were only a baby then."

"Well, I do!" Sadako said stubbornly.

After a speech by the mayor, hundreds of white doves were freed from their cages. Then, when the sun went down, a dazzling display of fireworks lit up the dark sky.

Afterward, everyone carried rice-paper lanterns to the banks of the Ohta River. Written on the rice paper were the names of relatives and friends who had died because of the Thunderbolt. Sadako had written Obasan's name on hers.

Candles were lit inside the lanterns. Then they were launched on the river, floating out to sea like a swarm of fireflies.

It was the beginning of autumn when Sadako rushed into the house with the good news.

"The most wonderful thing has happened!" she said breathlessly. "The big race on Field Day! I've been chosen to be on the relay team!" She danced around the room. "If we win, I'll be sure to get on the team next year!"

That was what Sadako wanted more than anything else.

From then on, Sadako thought of only one thing—the relay race. She practised every day at school and often ran all the way home. Masahiro timed her with their father's big watch.

Sadako dreamed of running faster. Maybe, she thought, I will be the best runner in the whole world.

At last the big day arrived. Parents, relatives, and friends gathered at the school to watch the sports events. Sadako was so nervous she was afraid her legs wouldn't work at all.

"Don't worry," Mrs. Sasaki said. "When you get out there, you will run as fast as you can."

At the signal to start, Sadako forgot everything but the race. When it was her turn, she ran with all the strength she had. Her heart thumped painfully against her ribs when the race was over.

It was then that a strange, dizzy feeling came over her. She scarcely heard when someone cried, "Sadako! Your team won!" The class surrounded Sadako, cheering and shouting. She shook her head a few times and the dizziness went away.

All winter long, Sadako practised to improve her speed. But every now and then the dizziness returned. She didn't tell anyone about it, not even Chizuko. Frightened, Sadako kept the secret inside of her.

On New Year's Eve, Mrs. Sasaki hung good-luck symbols above the door to protect her family all through the year.

"As soon as we can afford it, I'll buy a kimono for you," she promised Sadako. "A girl your age should have one."

Sadako politely thanked her mother, but she didn't care about a kimono. She only cared about racing with the team next year.

For several weeks it seemed that the good-luck symbols were working. Sadako felt strong and healthy, and she ran faster and faster.

But all that ended one crisp, cold winter day in February when Sadako was running in the school yard. Suddenly everything seemed to whirl around her, and she sank to the ground.

Soon Sadako was in an examining room in the hospital, where a nurse took some of her blood. Dr. Numata tapped her back and asked a lot of questions.

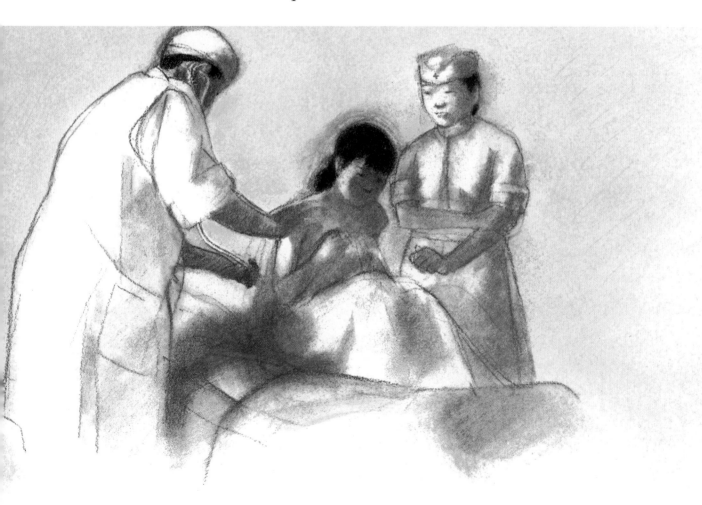

Sadako heard the doctor say the word "leukemia." That was the sickness caused by the atom bomb! She put her hands over her ears, not wanting to hear any more.

Mrs. Sasaki put her arms around Sadako. "You must stay here for a little while," she said. "But I'll come every evening."

"Do I really have the atom-bomb disease?" Sadako asked anxiously.

"The doctors want to take some tests, that's all," her father told her. "They might keep you here a few weeks."

A few weeks! To Sadako it seemed like years. What about the relay team?

When her family had left for the night, Sadako buried her face in the pillow and cried for a long time. She had never felt so lonely.

The next day, Chizuko came to visit, smiling mysteriously.

"Close your eyes," she said. Sadako held her eyes tightly shut. "Now you can look!"

Sadako stared at the paper and scissors on the bed. "What's that for?"

"I've figured out a way for you to get well," Chizuko said proudly. "Watch!"

She cut a piece of gold paper into a large square and folded it over and over, until it became a beautiful crane.

Sadako was puzzled. "But how can that paper bird make me well?"

"Don't you remember that old story about the crane?" Chizuko asked. "It's supposed to live for a thousand years. If a sick person folds one thousand cranes, the gods will grant her wish and make her well again."

She handed the golden crane to Sadako. "Here's your first one."

"Thank you, Chizuko chan," Sadako whispered. "I'll never part with it."

That night, Sadako felt safe and lucky. She set to work folding cranes, and Masahiro hung them from the ceiling. Why, in a few weeks she would be able to finish the thousand cranes and go home—all well again.

Eleven...I wish I'd get better...

Twelve...I wish I'd get better...

One day Nurse Yasunaga wheeled Sadako out onto the porch for some sunshine. There Sadako met Kenji. He was nine and small for his age, with a thin face and shining dark eyes.

Soon the two were talking like old friends. Kenji had been in the hospital for a long time, but his parents were dead and he had few visitors.

"It doesn't really matter," Kenji said with a sigh, "because I'll die soon. I have leukemia from the bomb."

Sadako didn't know what to say. She wanted so much to comfort him. Then she remembered. "You can make paper cranes like I do," she said, "so that a miracle can happen!"

"I know about the cranes," Kenji said quietly. "But it's too late. Even the gods can't help me now."

That night, Sadako folded a big crane out of her prettiest paper and sent it across the hall to Kenji's room. Perhaps it would bring him luck. Then she made more birds for her own flock.

One hundred ninety-eight...I wish I'd get better...

One hundred ninety-nine...I wish I'd get better...

One day Kenji didn't appear on the porch, and Sadako knew that Kenji had died.

Late that night, Sadako sat at the window, letting the tears come. After a while, she felt the nurse's gentle hand on her shoulder.

"Do you think Kenji is out there on a star island?" Sadako asked.

"Wherever he is, I'm sure he is happy now," the nurse replied. "He has shed that tired, sick body, and his spirit is free."

"I'm going to die next, aren't I?"

"Of course not!" Nurse Yasunaga answered with a firm shake of her head. "Come, let me see you fold another crane before you go to sleep. After you finish one thousand, you'll live to be an old, old lady."

Sadako tried hard to believe that. She folded birds and made the same wish. Now there were more than three hundred cranes.

In July it was warm and sunny, and Sadako seemed to be getting better.

"I'm over halfway to a thousand cranes," she told Masahiro, "so something good is going to happen."

And it did.

Her appetite came back and much of the pain went away. She was going to get to go home for O Bon, the biggest holiday of the year. O Bon was a special celebration for spirits of the dead who returned to visit their loved ones on earth.

Mrs. Sasaki and Mitsue had scrubbed and swept the house, and the air was filled with smells of delicious holiday food. Dishes of bean cakes and rice balls had been placed on the altar.

After they had eaten, Eiji handed Sadako a big box tied with a red ribbon. Slowly Sadako opened it. Inside was a silk kimono with cherry blossoms on it. Sadako felt hot tears blur her eyes.

"Why did you do it?" she asked, stroking the soft cloth. "Silk costs so much money."

"Sadako chan," her father said gently, "your mother stayed up late last night to finish sewing it. Try it on for her."

Mrs. Sasaki helped her put on the kimono and tie the sash. Everyone agreed that she looked like a princess.

Sadako let out a happy sigh. Perhaps—just perhaps—she was home to stay.

But by the end of the week Sadako was weak again and had to return to the hospital. The class sent her a Kokeshi doll to cheer her up. Sadako placed it on the bedside table next to the golden crane.

For the next few days, Sadako drifted in and out of a strange kind of half-sleep. Her parents sat beside the bed.

"When I die," she said dreamily, "will you put my favourite bean cakes on the altar for my spirit? And put a lantern on the Ohta River for me on Peace Day?"

Mrs. Sasaki could not speak. She took her daughter's hand and held it tightly.

"Hush!" Mr. Sasaki said. "That will not happen for many, many more years. Don't give up now, Sadako chan. You have to make only a few hundred more cranes."

As Sadako grew weaker, she wondered, Did it hurt to die? Or was it like falling asleep? Would she live on a heavenly mountain or star?

She fumbled with a piece of paper and clumsily folded one more bird.

Six hundred forty-four...

Her mother came in and felt her forehead. She gently took the paper away. As Sadako closed her eyes, she heard her mother whisper,

"O flock of heavenly cranes,
Cover my child with your wings."

When she opened her eyes again, Sadako saw her family there beside the bed. She looked around at their faces and smiled. She knew that she would always be a part of that warm, loving circle.

Sadako looked up at the flock of paper cranes hanging from the ceiling. As she watched, a light autumn breeze made the birds rustle and sway. They seemed to be alive, and flying out through the open window.

Sadako sighed and closed her eyes. How beautiful and free they were.

Sadako Sasaki died on October 25, 1955.

Her friends and classmates worked together to fold 356 paper cranes, so that she would be buried with one thousand. In a way, she got her wish. She will live on in the hearts of all the people who hear her story.

The class collected Sadako's letters and writings and published them in a book called *Kokeshi*, after the doll they had given her. A Folded Crane Club was organized in her honour.

Sadako's friends began to dream of a monument to her and all the children who were killed by the bomb. Young people throughout the country helped collect money. They wrote letters and shared Sadako's story. Finally, in 1958, their dream came true.

Now there is a statue of Sadako in Hiroshima Peace Park. She is standing on the Mountain of Paradise, holding a golden crane in out-stretched hands.

Every year, on Peace Day, children hang garlands of paper cranes under the statue. Their wish is engraved at its base:

This is our cry,
this is our prayer:
Peace in the world.

FOLLOW
UP

What was it about Sadako that inspired such love from her friends?

Understanding the Story

The Search for Peace

- When is Peace Day celebrated in Japan? Why?

- What happened to Sadako's grandmother? What does Sadako do as a memorial to her?

- What is the first clue in the story that something bad might happen to Sadako?

- What plan does Chizuko suggest to cheer up Sadako in hospital? Does the plan work for Sadako or her fellow patient, Kenji?

- Why do Sadako's friends go on folding cranes after she dies?

WRITER'S CRAFT

Symbols

Cranes are a multi-layered symbol in this story. What story does Chizuko tell about the cranes? What do the cranes symbolize to Sadako when she's ill? How does her attempt to fold one thousand cranes help her? When she's dying, what do the cranes symbolize to her? Finally, at the end of the story, children hang garlands of paper cranes on Sadako's statue. What do the cranes symbolize to today's children?

IMAGINE!
Your class has decided to celebrate Peace Day.
Will you fold paper cranes?
What other projects could you undertake?

Did You Know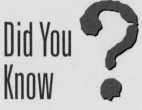

On August 6th, 1945, an American bomber dropped an atomic bomb on the Japanese city of Hiroshima. Three days later, they dropped another atom bomb on the city of Nagasaki. More than a hundred thousand people died immediately in these blasts, and others became ill years later from diseases caused by radiation. The destruction was so terrible that both sides ended the war, and most nations have now promised never to use another nuclear weapon. The city of Hiroshima is now a centre for peace.

Story Structure – Foreshadowing

The author, Eleanor Coerr, has skillfully built in to the story clues for the reader about what is going to happen to Sadako. The first one is on page 124, when we learn that Sadako was present when the atom bomb fell. This kind of clue is called **foreshadowing**. Find the other clues in the story that foretell Sadako's illness. How do these clues make you feel? Try using foreshadowing in a story you write.

Home Link

Origami: Fold a Crane

The Japanese craft of paper-folding (origami) has become popular in many countries. At your library, look for an origami book that has instructions for folding a crane. (You may want to start with easier projects, then work up to the crane!)

You and your classmates can make several crane garlands to hang in the classroom. Invite family members to visit the class, and share the story of Sadako with them.

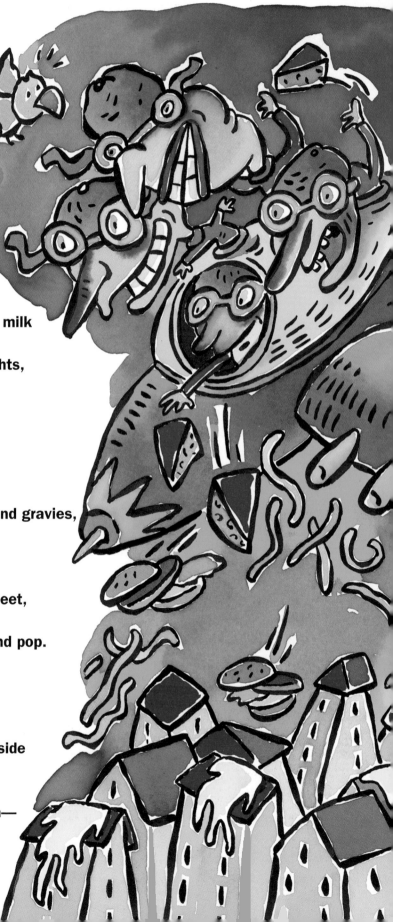

In the Next War

Poem by **Robert Priest**
Illustration by **Mohamed Danawi**

In the next war don't drop the bomb,
drop the excess wheat.
Drop the sacks of grain and powdered milk
we have too much of.
Send our best pilots over in daring flights,
their bombers full
of fish eggs, huge cheeses
and birthday cake icings.
Don't machine-gun our enemies—
Rather let us scrape off our plates
and pelt them with leftover squash.
We must inundate them with sauces and gravies,
each day a new and better recipe.
We have the technology to do this,
we have invisible aircraft.
Now we must make an undetectable fleet,
a silver sky train
that drops a mountain of TV dinners and pop.
Bury the enemy in spaghetti,
minute rice and mashed potatoes.
This will be a new kind of war.
It will take sacrifice and patience.
Everyone will have to put something aside
for the enemy,
starting with the ham and eggs,
saving for the very end our big weapon—
The hamburger!

Personal Response

- Did you enjoy poet Robert Priest's suggestions on how we should fight the next war?
- What are your favourite lines in the poem?
- Is there a serious message in this poem? What is it?
- Do you think humour is a good way to get people thinking? Explain.

A Slogan

Create a peace slogan based on the "food, not weapons" idea in Robert Priest's poem. A slogan should be short and snappy: quick to read, quick to make its point, and easy to remember. Here are some examples:

- Send pickles not missiles.
- Drive franks not tanks.

When you have invented a slogan you like, turn it into a button, a sign, a bumper sticker, a message on a T-shirt or baseball cap…or whatever you can think of!

MORE GOOD READING

On the Wings of Peace: Writers and Illustrators Speak Out for Peace in Memory of Hiroshima and Nagasaki edited by Sheila Hamanaka
Poems, stories, and images combine in this collection about the horror of conflict, and the wonder of peace. (an anthology)

❧ **Noguchi the Samurai by Burt Konzak**
A clever samurai shows his fellow passengers how to deal with a terrifying bully. (a picture book)

The Flame of Peace by Deborah Nourse Lattimore
This beautifully illustrated picture book tells the story of young Two Flint, and how he brings peace to his people. (an Aztec legend)

❧ **Oliver's Wars by Budge Wilson**
An award-winning story about Oliver, a young boy whose father has been sent overseas during the Gulf War. Oliver learns to handle his father's absence, and the taunts of other children. (a novel)

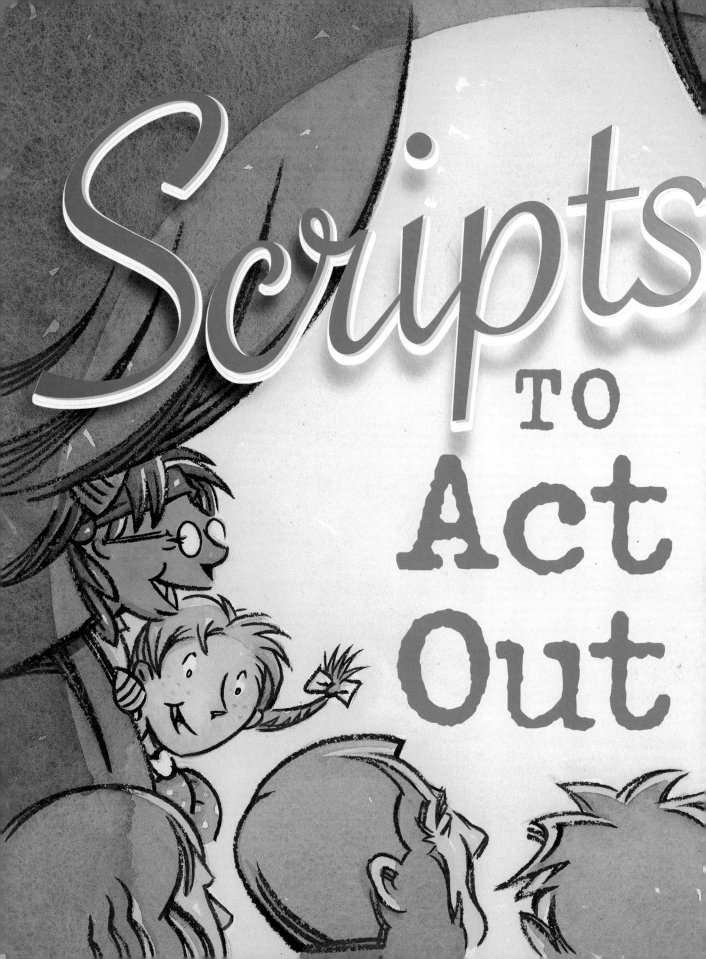

A Pizza the Size of the Sun

POEMS TO ACT OUT

by Jack Prelutsky

I Am Phoenix

POEMS FOR TWO VOICES

by Paul Fleischman

Windows on the World:

Plays and Activities Adapted from Folk Tales from Different Lands

by Sylvia Sikundar

Stories On Stage

Reader's Theatre Scripts

by Aaron Shepard

2 Poems

Performance
Poems by
Jack Prelutsky

Illustration by
Philippe Béha

Zeke McPeake

I'm Zeke McPeake,
and when I speak,
my voice is but
a teeny squeak.

No matter how
I try to shout,
I can't make more
than this come out.

If I should whisper,
strain your ears,
the volume almost
disappears.

I'm Zeke McPeake,
I talk this way,
so listen close—
I've much to say.

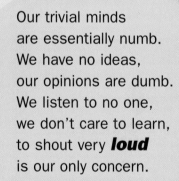

We're Loudies!

We're **Loudies**, *loud* **Loudies**!
We're **loud**, very **loud**.
Our overblown voices
stand out in a crowd.
We **yell** and we **yammer**,
we **bellow** and **bray**,
too dense to admit
that we've nothing to say.

We're **Loudies**, *loud* **Loudies**!
We never turn off.
We're **louder** than hogs
swilling slop from a trough.
We constantly **crow**.
We incessantly **shout**,
our only intention
is drowning you out.

Our trivial minds
are essentially numb.
We have no ideas,
our opinions are dumb.
We listen to no one,
we don't care to learn,
to shout very **loud**
is our only concern.

When *loud* **Loudies** meet,
we start wagging our tongues.
We open our throats
and we **shout** out our lungs.
We **bluster** and **boast**
until both of us burst—
no *loud* **Loudie** stops
till the other stops first!

Reflecting on *Scripts to Act Out*

This unit is designed to get you speaking out loud, even acting on a stage. So thinking about your voice is a good way to begin. If you normally speak quietly, you'll want to work on raising your voice so you can be heard. If you normally speak at top volume all the time, you'll want to work at varying the loudness of your voice to suit what you're saying.

Choral Reading

DRAMA WORKSHOP

Work with three or more classmates to perform a choral reading of one of these poems. Here are a few hints:

☆ *Zeke McPeake*: Work in a group of four. Have one person say each verse. Pay attention to the different voices Zeke uses in each verse.

RESPONDING
to 2 POEMS

Personal Response

• Do you identify more with Zeke McPeake and his tiny voice, or with the loud Loudies? Explain your answer.
• Do you know people like Zeke or the Loudies? What do you like about them? What do you dislike?

☆ *We're Loudies!*: Work in a large group. Pay special attention to the words in **boldface** type, and change your volume as you read. Remember, your performance will be boring if all the verses are shouted in the same way!

Acting Tip 1

Think of the People in the Back Row

If you want to be heard by everyone in the audience, you must **speak up!** You don't want people in the back row to miss the whole show; remember that they could be sitting beside a chattering child, or behind a crying baby.

Not speaking loudly or clearly enough is the most common fault of amateur actors. So practise **projecting your voice** in the gym or auditorium in your school. Recite a verse from *We're Loudies!* Pronounce each word clearly and slowly. Have your group members sit at the back of the room. They'll let you know if they can hear you clearly!

Projecting your voice means to speak out so that your voice can be heard at a distance. This involves volume as well as clear speech, but does not mean your words are shouted. Professional actors are able to speak in a normal voice to the very back row, without shouting.

A Performance Poem

Write a performance poem that will give you and your classmates more opportunities to stretch and exercise your voices. Your poem could focus on a different way of speaking—high, low, fast, slow, soft, harsh, and so on—or on different emotions—excitement, joy, anger, love, and so on. Here are some sample first lines:

- I'm Elly McSqueak, and when I speak…
- We're Fasties, *fast* Fasties!…

TECH LINK

Use a word-processing program to help you play with your poem—just as Jack Prelutsky has. You can change the size or style of the letters to emphasize certain words or lines.

Too Young For This;

Make two lists of things that someone has told you you're "too young" or "too old" for. Read on, and compare your lists with the complaints of the narrator in the monologue.

Monologue by
Peg Kehret

Illustration by
Kathryn Adams

monologue: a speech for one actor. Professional actors often perform monologues when they audition for a part.

I am presently in what the psychologists refer to as **The Awkward Age.** That means I'm not a little kid any longer, but I'm not grown-up yet, either. It also means that my parents can't decide which category I belong in. The result of their indecision is very confusing, and if they aren't careful, I'm going to end up needing one of those psychologists.

For example, according to my mother, I am too old for many of the activities I still enjoy. I am too old to go trick-or-treating on Halloween. I am too old to spy on my sister when she comes home from a date. I am too old to swipe apples from Mrs. Munster's tree.

Besides being too old, I am also old enough to know better. *(Mimic a scolding adult:)* "*(Name)* _____! You are old enough to know better than to wear those muddy shoes on the carpet.*" "*(Name)* _____! You are old enough to know better than to let the parakeet out of his cage when the cat's indoors." *(Helpless shrug.)*

On the other hand, I am much too young for many of the things I would like to do. According to my parents, I am too young to attend an unchaperoned party. I am too young to go shopping downtown alone. I am too young to attend a movie that's rated PG unless my mother has read a review of it.

The bad part about all this is that there is no reasonable explanation for which things I'm too old for and which I'm too young for. I never know what to expect. Now, I am not an unreasonable person. Nor am I stupid. I know I'm too young to get married, and I know I'm too old to pick my nose in public. I do have some common sense. But no one—least of all my parents—gives me credit for that.

Too Old For That!

My father says, "You are old enough to do your share of the work around here."

My mother says, "You are much too young to run the power lawn mower alone."

He says, "Can't you read anything but comic books? You're old enough to stretch your mind a little."

"She says, "Where on earth did you get that book? You're too young to read that sort of thing."

Do you know what I think? I think my parents are trying too hard to raise the perfect kid. And the next time they say I'm too young for this or too old for that, I plan to tell them so.

"You think I'm going to turn out perfect?" I'll say. "Ha! You're old enough to know better." ◆

RESPONDING

to TOO YOUNG FOR THIS; TOO OLD FOR THAT!

FOLLOW UP

How do your lists of things you're "too young" or "too old" for compare with the narrator's. Which of the narrator's points hits home the most?

Understanding the Monologue

Old Enough...

- Do you think the narrator is justified when he/she says: "There is no reasonable explanation for which things I'm too old for and which I'm too young for"? Explain your answer.
- In your opinion, does the ending make an effective "punch line" for the monologue? Explain your answer.

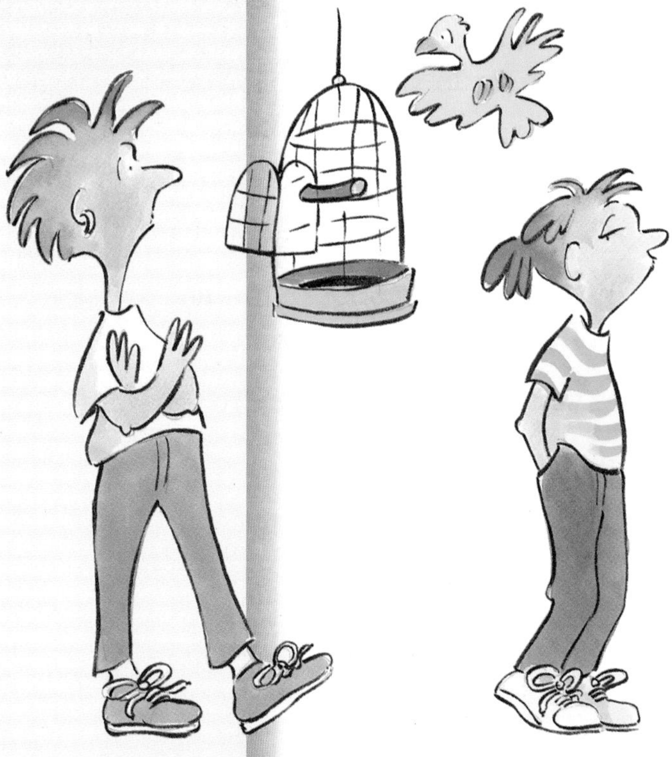

Improvisation

DRAMA WORKSHOP

A good way to get into the spirit of acting is to improvise. When you improvise, you don't use a script. Instead, you think of a situation and a role to play, then just make up the speeches to suit. There are several possible scenes in the monologue that you and a friend or two could improvise. For example:

☆ the mother catches the narrator letting the parakeet out of its cage
☆ the narrator spies on the sister
☆ the narrator talks to both parents about doing chores
☆ another scene of your choice

Monologue

DRAMA WORKSHOP

Review Acting Tips 1 and 2 (page 141 and this page) and then prepare a dramatic reading of the monologue. Follow these steps:

1. Decide whether or not you'll memorize the monologue.
2. Get inside your character. Actors try to become the person they're playing.
3. Think about how to use your voice expressively. Work on different voices: one for you, one for the mother, and one for the father.
4. Look up any words you don't know. You should understand everything you're saying.
5. Practise, practise, practise! so that you can read or recite the monologue without stumbling.
6. Perform the monologue for the class, or family members. Ask them for feedback on your performance.

To make your performance unique, consider the following variations:

☆ Wear a costume.
☆ Use props, such as movie tickets or comic books.
☆ Add sound effects and turn the monologue into a radio play.
☆ Write your own monologue with the same title, but your personal list of things you're "too young" and "too old" for.

Acting Tip 2

Slow Down!

You want to be a great actor, right? Then take your time when you're speaking: don't rush through all your lines like a runaway train. As you say the lines, take time to think about the words and what they mean. But *don't* say every line slowly. Use different speeds as you speak—slow down some lines, say others quickly. Your lines shouldn't sound like something you've memorized. They should sound as though you've *just* thought of the words.

When you perform the monologue, ask your audience for feedback about how well you're doing at speaking slowly, clearly, and expressively.

This TV script is a Heritage Minute, one of a series of short films about Canadian history. Read the first set of camera directions to find out the setting (time and place) and the situation (who the people are, what they are doing).

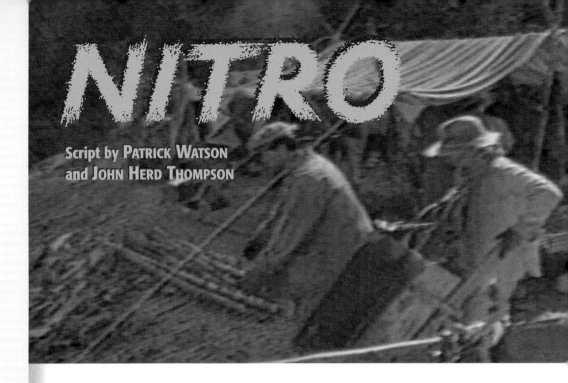

NITRO

Script by PATRICK WATSON and JOHN HERD THOMPSON

Outdoor scene is a long shot of working camp; workers are dumping rocks from wheelbarrow down cliff side. Horses are pulling carts. There's a tent, at centre, in which Chinese workers are gathered. Sound effects of rocks crashing into each other, hammering, workers talking, shouting, horses neighing, which fade out as we cut to medium shot of Cochrane, who is approaching tent. On-screen the following text appears as caption: **The Building of the CP Railroad, 1884.**

Media Glossary

long shot: camera is set far away from action; viewer sees larger scene

medium shot: camera is closer to action; viewer sees only part of larger scene

close-up: camera is very close to subject; viewer sees only one part of scene, such as hands lifting vial

cut to: camera shifts quickly from one scene to another

off-screen: actor's voice is heard, but he or she is not seen

Cochrane: Alright! Who wants to earn some danger pay? Boat fare for the wife. All you have to do is go down in the tunnel with the nitro and set the charge.

Cut to Leung, standing among other workers, looking eager. Leung moves forward to volunteer.

Leung: My wife? You pay boat? OK, OK! I do, I do really good, you see.

Cut to Cochrane and Leung. Cut to close-up of hands pulling vial of nitro from box. Hands pass nitro to Leung. Cut to Leung moving away. Cut to inside of tunnel, can see opening and Leung approaching, walking carefully.

Hear Cochrane saying off-screen:

Cochrane: Now, pour it in the hole gently. Understand? **Cut to Cochrane and Smith. Cut to other workers, looking anxious.** Any little **bump** and that stuff will blo...

Sound effects of explosion as camera cuts back to explosion in tunnel. Cut to workers holding up their arms protectively. Cut to rocks flying from tunnel. Cut to Smith and Cochrane.

Smith: That's the third one we've lost this month! Cochrane, get another volunteer.

Smith walks away. Cut to tunnel. Leung, battered and covered in black, walks out of tunnel. Cut to faces of relieved fellow workers. Cut to Leung waving. Off-screen we hear voice of Leung, years later; sounds of camp fade out.

Leung: I went back in again. **Cut to Leung fifty years after explosion. On-screen the following text appears as caption: Vancouver 50 years later. This is long shot of older Leung with grandchildren.** But I lost many friends. They say there is one dead Chinese man for every mile of that track. That's what they say. ◆

Before you read this script, how much did you know about the contributions of Chinese people in building Canada's railroad? What new things did you learn from this TV script?

Understanding the Script

Working on the Railroad

- What is nitro? What is it used for? Why is it dangerous?
- Why does Leung accept the dangerous assignment of planting the nitro?
- How do you think Leung escapes being killed?
- Fifty years later, what feelings does Leung have about his job building the Canadian Pacific Railroad?

Camera Directions

GROUP DISCUSSION

Reread the media glossary and the directions in this TV script. With four or five classmates, discuss why the camera operator is such an important person in the making of a TV show. Who else is involved in the production of a show? What do their jobs involve?

Tableau Vivant

DRAMA WORKSHOP

A *tableau vivant* is a living presentation of a picture or scene formed by a group of actors posing silently and motionlessly. With a group, practise and present a tableau vivant of an important moment in *Nitro*, such as

- ☆ Leung's fellow workers beg him not to take on the dangerous job, but he brushes them away
- ☆ the other workers show surprise, shock, and joy when they hear Leung's voice after the explosion

Experiment with poses and facial expressions until you are satisfied that you're capturing the moment. Then all together freeze—stay motionless for at least five seconds. Ask someone to take a photograph, and evaluate your performance.

Acting Tip 3

All Great Actors "Cheat"

When you're on stage, should you always face the audience so that they can see your face and hear your words? Or should you face the other actors, so that it looks as if you're carrying on a natural conversation? Well, good actors learn to "cheat," which means they stand so that they're half-turned toward the other actors, and half-turned toward their audience. The audience can see and hear them clearly, but it still looks like they are having a natural conversation with the other actors.

Try "cheating" next time you're on stage with other actors—in your tableau vivant, for example.

Media Link Heritage Minutes

Think of what happens in this script from a Heritage Minute. Now think of a moment in Canadian history that you would like to record as a Heritage Minute. Use *Nitro* as a model, and write a script. If you have the video equipment, you could record your script. Or perform it live for your classmates.

Preview the script for *The Tiger's Whisker*. The words in **italic** are called **stage directions**. They inform the actors about what they should be doing on the stage. As you read, imagine what the characters look like and what they're doing in between their speeches.

Stage Play by
SYLVIA SIKUNDAR

Illustrations by
BARBARA SPURLL

mouse deer: a small antelope-like animal, about half a metre high, that lives in the forests of Indonesia

The Tiger's Whisker

Cast of Characters

Tiger King

Tiger Adviser 1, 2, and 3

Tiger Officer (4 or more)

Hornbills (8 or more)

Mouse Deer 1 and 2

Porcupine

Note that when performing this play, boys or girls could take any of the roles (the Tiger King could be a Tiger Queen).

The Tiger King is pacing back and forth across the stage. Three Tiger Advisers watch him.

Tiger King: I have sent tigers all over the island in search of food and they come back with nothing. What can I do? I have a responsibility to my subjects! They're going to starve. You're my advisers. What do you suggest I do?

The three Tiger Advisers talk among themselves.

Tiger King: Hurry up! I'm waiting.

Tiger Adviser 1: We must examine the facts of the matter, Your Majesty.

Tiger King: Yes? And what are they?

Tiger Adviser 2: Fact number one: There are very few animals left on this island for us to hunt.

Tiger King: Don't waste my time! We know that already!

Tiger Adviser 3: Fact number two: There are over 13 000 islands in the Indonesian archipelago, of which this island is only one.

Tiger King: What does it matter to us how many islands there are in the Indonesian archipelago? We're tigers, we can't swim to other islands. And I don't suppose the animals we hunt are going to swim to us.

Tiger Adviser 1 *(with a fake, polite laugh):* Yes, Your Majesty, that is true. You are, as usual, right in all things. But Your Majesty is so powerful... Why don't you command someone other than a tiger to make a scouting trip to the nearby islands?

Tiger King: Yes, why don't I?

Tiger Adviser 2: Bring in the Hornbills!

Tiger Officers hustle Hornbills onto the stage.

Tiger Adviser 3: These are Hornbills, Your Majesty. May we suggest you command each one of them to fly in a different direction. The first to return with information about animals for us to hunt on another island will receive a generous reward—to be determined by Your Majesty, of course.

Tiger King: Yes, yes! That's good. *(to the Hornbills)* You've heard your instructions. There's no time to waste! My stomach is grumbling! Depart at once!

The Hornbills "fly" off on their scouting trip. After a short interval, one Hornbill runs on stage and drops onto its knees before the Tiger King.

Hornbill *(out of breath):* Your Majesty, I have good news. An island not very far from here has an abundance of juicy mouse deer. They could provide food for Your Majesty and your subjects for a long time.

Tiger King: Really? *(He looks around, pleased. The Tiger Advisers and Tiger Officers express their delight.)* Where is this island?

Hornbill: Just to the east.

Tiger King: Is it the island we can see from here?

Hornbill: Yes, Your Majesty.

Tiger Adviser 1: It is close enough, Your Majesty, for us to build a bridge of stones to reach it.

Tiger King: Build the bridge immediately. My officers will carry a message to the king of that island, telling him to send food to us immediately. If he refuses, we will invade the island and take what we want for ourselves.

Tiger Advisers and Tiger Officers: Yes, Your Majesty.

The Tiger Advisers and Tiger Officers lay down a series of "stones" for the bridge. To get to the island to the east, the Tiger Officers will hop along from stone to stone.

Tiger King: Is it ready?

Tiger Advisers and Tiger Officers: Yes, Your Majesty.

Tiger King: When you deliver my message, I want you to strike fear into all who listen. Take this whisker of mine with you. I want the king of the island to the east to know how great and powerful I am.

The Tiger King "plucks" one of his whiskers. The Tiger Advisers and Tiger Officers gasp, then sigh with relief when it's clear the Tiger King is not in pain.

Tiger King: Here! Take it!

Tiger Advisers and Tiger Officers: Yes, Your Majesty.

The Tiger King and Tiger Advisers exit. The three Tiger Officers make their military-style crossing to the other island with the Hornbill in the lead.

Tiger Officer 1: We're here! But I don't see anyone.

Hornbill: Sssh! Here they come now!

Two Mouse Deer enter.

Mouse Deer 1 *(trying to hide its trembling):* Hello!

Tiger Officer 1: Greetings! We bring a message from the great Tiger King of the island to the west.

Tiger Officer 2: Where is your king? We must deliver the message directly to him.

Mouse Deer 2 *(looking anxiously at Mouse Deer 1):* We don't have a king.

Tiger Officer 3: You don't have a king?

Mouse Deer 1 *(nudging Mouse Deer 2):* What my fellow Mouse Deer means is we are ruled by a queen not a king.

Tiger Officer 3: All right. Where is your queen?

Mouse Deer 1: She's having a nap.

Tiger Officer 2: Well, wake her up! We must deliver this message to her right away. Where can we find her?

Mouse Deer 1: Our queen will be very angry if you wake her up. She doesn't like strangers. I suggest you let me take the message to her for you.

The three Tiger Officers discuss this among themselves.

Tiger Officer 3: All right, you may take the message to her for us.

Tiger Officer 1: This is our king's demand. Your queen must send food for all his subjects to his island immediately. If your queen refuses, our king will invade this island.

Mouse Deer 2: Oh, no!

Mouse Deer 1: I will deliver the message to our queen and bring you her answer. Rest here until I return. My friend will bring you some cool coconut milk for refreshment.

Hornbill: I'll come with you.

Mouse Deer 1: You're a bird. It will be difficult for you to run swiftly along the forest path with me, and you won't be able to see me from the air.

Hornbill: That's true.

Mouse Deer 1: Please be patient. I will return immediately.

Tiger Officer 2: All right. We'll wait. But return quickly with your queen's answer.

Mouse Deer 1: I will, I will. Rest in the shade of those trees *(points off-stage)*. I'll bring the answer soon.

Tiger Officer 1: Just one more thing. Our king sent this whisker to show how great and powerful he is. It is from his royal visage. Please take it to your queen along with our message.

Tiger Officer 2: We'll have a look around those rice fields while we're waiting.

The Tiger Officers give Mouse Deer 1 the whisker and with the Hornbill follow Mouse Deer 2 off-stage.

Mouse Deer 1: What am I going to do? If the king sends his army to invade our island, he will want meat. And I'm meat.

Porcupine enters.

Porcupine: Hello, Mouse Deer.

Mouse Deer 1: Hello, Porcupine. I'm so glad you've come. Something terrible has happened! The Tiger King from the island to the west says he will invade our island immediately if we don't send him enough food for him and all his subjects.

Porcupine: What kind of food does he want?

Mouse Deer 1: Meat! Meat! Tigers eat meat. To a tiger I'm lunch and dinner. This *(waving the whisker)* is the Tiger King's whisker.

Porcupine *(trembling):* It looks as if it came from a very large tiger.

Mouse Deer 1: It sure does. *(shivers)*

Porcupine: What are you going to do?

Mouse Deer 1: I don't know. At least you've got weapons. *(It looks enviously at Porcupine's quills.)* Hmmm…that gives me an idea. Will you give me one of your longest quills?

Porcupine: Of course. I'll help you in any way I can. *(It reaches behind its back and pulls out the longest quill.)* Here you go. What are you going to do with it?

Mouse Deer 1 *(measuring the quill against the whisker):* You tell me, Porcupine. If this is from a great Tiger King *(holding up the whisker)*, how large a creature would you say *this* is from *(holding up the quill)*?

Porcupine: A very large one! You're so clever!

Mouse Deer 1: Let me go and get rid of these three brave tigers from the island to the west.

Porcupine *(while exiting):* Good luck!

Mouse Deer 2 *(running in from the opposite direction):* Mouse Deer! Watch out! They're coming! They wouldn't wait any longer.

The Tiger Officers and the Hornbill enter from the same direction as Mouse Deer 2.

Tiger Officer 1: Well, Mouse Deer! Did you deliver the message?

Mouse Deer 1: Yes! Yes, I did.

Tiger Officer 2: What was your queen's response? Tell us immediately.

Mouse Deer 1: Our queen sends greetings to the Tiger King of the island to the west.

Tiger Officer 1: As she should.

Tiger Officer 2: What else did she say?

Mouse Deer 1: She regrets that she must tell you she is unable to send your king any food.

Tiger Officer 3: What?

Tiger Officer 2: How dare she? Did you give her our king's whisker? Didn't she see how mighty he is?

Mouse Deer 1: Yes, of course I gave her the whisker. Our queen likes to receive presents. She also likes to give them. She would like to give this to your king in return.

Mouse Deer 1 hands the quill to Tiger Officer 3.

Tiger Officer 3: What's this?

Mouse Deer 1: It's one of our queen's whiskers.

Tiger Officer 2: But it's so large!

Mouse Deer 1 *(laughing):* Our queen has many whiskers larger than that one.

The Tiger Officers and the Hornbill look at one another in fear.

Tiger Officer 1: Please excuse us. We must return to our island immediately.

Mouse Deer 2 *(very sweetly):* Are you sure you wouldn't like some more coconut milk?

Tiger Officer 2: No! No! We're afraid not. We're in a hurry. Goodbye, Mouse Deer.

The Tiger Officers and the Hornbill exit in a hurry across the stone bridge.

Mouse Deer 1 *(laughing):* That scared them off. They won't come here again.

Mouse Deer 2: You're a genius! ◆

FOLLOW UP

What role would you like to play in a staged presentation of *The Tiger's Whisker*? Or would you rather make costumes, collect props, be the director, or prepare publicity materials? There will be a job for everyone!

Stage Play

DRAMA WORKSHOP

Follow these steps to perform *The Tiger's Whisker.*

1. Clear the desks from an area near the door to create a stage (or use the school's stage).
2. For the set, paint an island mural on large pieces of mural paper.
3. Choose someone to design and make simple masks or costumes for the animal characters.
4. Collect props such as stepping stones, the whisker, and the quill.
5. Select a director to tell the actors what to do.
6. Assign the acting parts. Review the Acting Tips!
7. Hold several rehearsals before you plan to perform the play (reading it from the text, or memorizing and then performing all the lines).
8. Make a poster to advertise the play. You'll want a good audience!

Acting Tip 4

Listen For Your Cue!

Professional actors listen and watch carefully to what other actors are saying or doing, so they'll know when to speak their lines. By paying close attention, they never miss their cue and say their line too early, or too late. A **cue** is the signal (another actor's last words, a ringing doorbell) that tells actors it's their turn to speak. It's a good idea to breathe in as soon as you hear your cue, so you'll have enough breath to say your line.

Acting Tip 5

Learn Your Stage Directions

It's important for all actors to know what they should be doing while on the stage. That's why **stage directions** are part of the script. Directors interpret stage directions, deciding exactly when, how, and where the actors should move.

A stage is divided into nine sections (see the diagram below), and directors will tell the actors where to stand or move by referring to these sections. For example, your director may tell you to come onto the stage down left, and then move to centre to deliver your line, and then move off stage up right. (Note that left and right on stage are determined from the actors' viewpoint, not the audience's.)

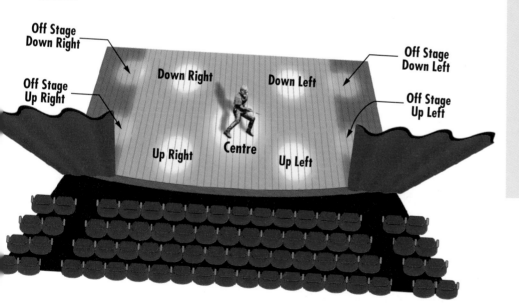

Off Stage Down Right

Off Stage Up Right

Off Stage Down Left

Off Stage Up Left

Down Right

Down Left

Up Right

Centre

Up Left